FORWARD/COMMENTARY

This document is intended for government officials responsible for implementing Homeland Security Presidential Directive-12 (HSPD-12) compliant physical access control systems (PACS). Information in this document is also useful to government contractors and physical security vendors that provide HSPD-12 systems, products, and integration services. It is expected that readers have a general knowledge of PIV standards, including FIPS 201-2, SP800-73, and SP800-78.

The National Institute of Standards and Technology (NIST) is a measurement standards laboratory, and a non-regulatory agency of the United States Department of Commerce. Its mission is to promote innovation and industrial competitiveness. Founded in 1901, as the National Bureau of Standards, NIST was formed with the mandate to provide standard weights and measures, and to serve as the national physical laboratory for the United States. With a world-class measurement and testing laboratory encompassing a wide range of areas of computer science, mathematics, statistics, and systems engineering, NIST's cybersecurity program supports its overall mission to promote U.S. innovation and industrial competitiveness by advancing measurement science, standards, and related technology through research and development in ways that enhance economic security and improve our quality of life.

The need for cybersecurity standards and best practices that address interoperability, usability and privacy has been shown to be critical for the nation. NIST's cybersecurity programs seek to enable greater development and application of practical, innovative security technologies and methodologies that enhance the country's ability to address current and future computer and information security challenges.

The cybersecurity publications produced by NIST cover a wide range of cybersecurity concepts that are carefully designed to work together to produce a holistic approach to cybersecurity primarily for government agencies and constitute the best practices used by industry. This holistic strategy to cybersecurity covers the gamut of security subjects from development of secure encryption standards for communication and storage of information while at rest to how best to recover from a cyber-attack.

Why buy a book you can download for free?   We print this so you don't have to.

We at 4th Watch Publishing are former government employees, so we know how government employees actually use the standards. When a new standard is released, an engineer prints it out, punches holes and puts it in a 3-ring binder. While this is not a big deal for a 5 or 10-page document, many NIST documents are over 100 pages and printing a large document is a time-consuming effort. So, an engineer that's paid $75 an hour is spending hours simply printing out the tools needed to do the job. That's time that could be better spent doing engineering. We publish these documents so engineers can focus on what they were hired to do – engineering. It's much more cost-effective to just order the latest version from Amazon.com If there is a standard you would like published, let us know. Our web site is www.usgovpub.com

Below are some other facility related books we publish on Amazon.com:

UFC 4-010-06	Cybersecurity of Facility-Related Control Systems
NIST SP 800-82	Guide to Industrial Control Systems (ICS) Security
NISTIR 8170	The Cybersecurity Framework
NISTIR 8089	An Industrial Control System Cybersecurity Performance Testbed
NIST SP 800-31	Intrusion Detection Systems
NIST SP 800-94	Guide to Intrusion Detection and Prevention Systems (IDPS)
NIST SP 1800-7	Situational Awareness for Electric Utilities
NISTIR 7628	Guidelines for Smart Grid Cybersecurity
DoD	Energy Manager's Handbook
FEMP	Operations & Maintenance Best Practices
UFC 4-020-01	DoD Security Engineering Facilities Planning Manual
UFC 4-021-02	Electronic Security Systems
GSA	GSA Courtroom Technology Manual
Draft NISTIR 8179	Criticality Analysis Process Model
NISTIR 8144	Assessing Threats to Mobile Devices & Infrastructure
NISTIR 8151	Dramatically Reducing Software Vulnerabilities
NIST SP 800-183	Networks of 'Things'
NIST SP 800-184	Guide for Cybersecurity Event Recovery
Whitepaper	NIST Framework for Improving Critical Infrastructure Cybersecurity

NIST Special Publication 800-116 Revision 1

Guidelines for the Use of PIV Credentials in Facility Access

Hildegard Ferraiolo
Ketan Mehta
Nabil Ghadiali
Jason Mohler
Vincent Johnson
Steven Brady

This publication is available free of charge from:
https://doi.org/10.6028/NIST.SP.800-116r1

INFORMATION SECURITY

National Institute of
Standards and Technology
U.S. Department of Commerce

NIST Special Publication 800-116
Revision 1

Guidelines for the Use of PIV Credentials in Facility Access

Hildegard Ferraiolo
Ketan Mehta
Computer Security Division
Information Technology Laboratory

Nabil Ghadiali
National Gallery of Art
Washington, DC

Jason Mohler
Vincent Johnson
Steven Brady
Electrosoft Services, Inc.
Reston, Virginia

This publication is available free of charge from:
https://doi.org/10.6028/NIST.SP.800-116r1

June 2018

U.S. Department of Commerce
Wilbur L. Ross, Jr., Secretary

National Institute of Standards and Technology
Walter Copan, NIST Director and Under Secretary of Commerce for Standards and Technology

Authority

This publication has been developed by NIST in accordance with its statutory responsibilities under the Federal Information Security Modernization Act (FISMA) of 2014, 44 U.S.C. § 3551 *et seq.*, Public Law (P.L.) 113-283. NIST is responsible for developing information security standards and guidelines, including minimum requirements for federal information systems, but such standards and guidelines shall not apply to national security systems without the express approval of appropriate federal officials exercising policy authority over such systems. This guideline is consistent with the requirements of the Office of Management and Budget (OMB) Circular A-130.

Nothing in this publication should be taken to contradict the standards and guidelines made mandatory and binding on federal agencies by the Secretary of Commerce under statutory authority. Nor should these guidelines be interpreted as altering or superseding the existing authorities of the Secretary of Commerce, Director of the OMB, or any other federal official. This publication may be used by nongovernmental organizations on a voluntary basis and is not subject to copyright in the United States. Attribution would, however, be appreciated by NIST.

National Institute of Standards and Technology Special Publication 800-116 Revision 1
Natl. Inst. Stand. Technol. Spec. Publ. 800-116 Revision 1, 71 pages (June 2018)
CODEN: NSPUE2

This publication is available free of charge from:
https://doi.org/10.6028/NIST.SP.800-116r1

Certain commercial entities, equipment, or materials may be identified in this document in order to describe an experimental procedure or concept adequately. Such identification is not intended to imply recommendation or endorsement by NIST, nor is it intended to imply that the entities, materials, or equipment are necessarily the best available for the purpose.

There may be references in this publication to other publications currently under development by NIST in accordance with its assigned statutory responsibilities. The information in this publication, including concepts and methodologies, may be used by federal agencies even before the completion of such companion publications. Thus, until each publication is completed, current requirements, guidelines, and procedures, where they exist, remain operative. For planning and transition purposes, Federal agencies may wish to closely follow the development of these new publications by NIST.

Organizations are encouraged to review all draft publications during public comment periods and provide feedback to NIST. Many NIST cybersecurity publications, other than the ones noted above, are available at https://csrc.nist.gov/publications.

Comments on this publication may be submitted to:

National Institute of Standards and Technology
Attn: Computer Security Division, Information Technology Laboratory
100 Bureau Drive (Mail Stop 8930) Gaithersburg, MD 20899-8930
Email: piv_comments@nist.gov

All comments are subject to release under the Freedom of Information Act (FOIA).

Reports on Computer Systems Technology

The Information Technology Laboratory (ITL) at the National Institute of Standards and Technology (NIST) promotes the U.S. economy and public welfare by providing technical leadership for the Nation's measurement and standards infrastructure. ITL develops tests, test methods, reference data, proof of concept implementations, and technical analyses to advance the development and productive use of information technology. ITL's responsibilities include the development of management, administrative, technical, and physical standards and guidelines for the cost-effective security and privacy of other than national security-related information in federal information systems. The Special Publication 800-series reports on ITL's research, guidelines, and outreach efforts in information system security, and its collaborative activities with industry, government, and academic organizations.

Abstract

This recommendation provides a technical guideline to use Personal Identity Verification (PIV) Cards in facility access; enabling federal agencies to operate as government-wide interoperable enterprises. These guidelines cover the risk-based strategy to select appropriate PIV authentication mechanisms as expressed within Federal Information Processing Standard (FIPS) 201.

Keywords

credential; e-authentication; identity credential; issuance; personal identity verification (PIV); physical access control system (PACS); PIV authentication mechanisms; PIV cards; public key infrastructure (PKI); validation

Acknowledgements

The authors of SP 800-116 Revision 1 (Hildegard Ferraiolo of NIST; Nabil Ghadiali of the
National Gallery of Art; and Jason Mohler, Vincent Johnson, and Steven Brady of Electrosoft
Services, Inc.) wish to thank William MacGregor, Ketan Mehta, and Karen Scarfone for their
substantial contribution towards the original version of this publication, and David Cooper for
his substantial contribution towards both the original version of this publication and the draft
version of this revision. The authors also gratefully acknowledge and appreciate the support and
contributions by many others in the public and private sectors whose helpful and beneficial
comments greatly enhance the utility of this publication. Special thanks to the Interagency
Security Committee (ISC), the General Services Administration, the Department of Homeland
Security, the Department of Defense, and the Office of Management and Budget for their review
and contributions to this document.

Audience

This document is intended for government officials responsible for implementing Homeland
Security Presidential Directive-12 (HSPD-12) compliant physical access control systems
(PACS). Information in this document is also useful to government contractors and physical
security vendors that provide HSPD-12 systems, products, and integration services. It is expected
that readers have a general knowledge of PIV standards, including [FIPS 201-2], [SP800-73],
and [SP800-78].

Executive Summary

Homeland Security Presidential Directive-12 [HSPD-12] sets a clear goal to improve federal facility access through the use of government-wide identity standards. These goals are reflected in the Office of Management and Budget (OMB) Circular A-130, which references SP 800-116 to ensure continued deployment and use of the identity credentials accessing Federal facilities.[1]

Federal Information Processing Standard 201 [FIPS201] defines characteristics of the identity credential that can be interoperable government-wide. In the context of [HSPD-12], the term *interoperability* means the ability to use any Personal Identity Verification (PIV) Card with any application performing one or more PIV authentication mechanisms. [FIPS201] also defines authentication mechanisms at four assurance levels (LITTLE or NO, SOME, HIGH, and VERY HIGH). These levels provide for the risk based approach as directed in HSPD-12 to "*include graduated criteria, from least secure to most secure, to ensure flexibility in selecting the appropriate level of security for each application.*"

The risk-based approach for facility access is stipulated via the designation of "Controlled, Limited, Exclusion" areas (see Section 4.3). Specifically, this document recommends PIV authentication mechanisms for "Controlled, Limited, Exclusion" in terms of authentication factors as shown in Table ES-1. Some agencies may have different names for their security areas, however each agency should establish their criteria to implement authentication consistent with this document.

Table ES-1 - Authentication Factors for Security Areas

Security Areas	Minimum Number of Authentication Factors Required
Controlled	1
Limited	2
Exclusion	3

[FIPS201] identifies a number of authentication mechanisms supported by mandatory features of PIV Cards. These mechanisms include Authentication using Authentication with the Card Authentication Certificate Credential (PKI-CAK), Authentication Using Off-Card Biometric Comparison (BIO), Attended Authentication Using Off-Card Biometric Comparison (BIO-A), Authentication with the PIV Authentication Certificate Credential (PKI-AUTH). In addition, PIV Cards may optionally support a number of other authentication mechanisms; these include Authentication with the Symmetric Card Authentication Key (SYM-CAK) and Authentication Using On-Card Biometric Comparison (OCC-AUTH). Access points should not rely solely on an

---

[1] The OMB Circular A-130 can be located at
https://www.whitehouse.gov/sites/whitehouse.gov/files/omb/circulars/A130/a130revised.pdf.

authentication mechanism that requires optional card features as it is not guaranteed that the optional features to be used for authentication are present on all cards.

Many changes in this document were made to align SP 800-116 with revision 2 of FIPS 201 (FIPS 201-2). For example, credential validation is now required (see Section 4.4). The CHUID authentication mechanism has been deprecated due to security concerns. For this reason, this publication marks the authentication mechanism as deprecated to signify that it is not a viable authentication mechanism to deploy for physical access control system (PACS). The CHUID data element on the PIV Card, however, remains a mandatory element as the BIO(-A) and SYM-CAK authentication mechanisms use the data element as a source for the card's expiration date. It also provides unique identifiers for PACS ACLs. The previous version of this document also included the combined VIS + CHUID authentication mechanism as an option to transitioning from Unrestricted to Controlled areas. VIS + CHUID, however, is not included in this version of the document since it provides "LITTLE or NO" confidence in the identity of the cardholder.

Other changes in this version of the guideline include the removal of the migration strategy as PACS implementation in the Federal Government have moved beyond the described strategy and are more advanced. The future topics (i.e., global identifier and secure biometric match on card) have been addressed in FIPS 201-2 and associated technical specification and thus have become part of this version of guidelines rather than topics for future considerations. Finally, a new Appendix C describes possible improvements to PKI authentication for fast contactless transaction at access points. Appendix I, Revision History, provides a list of changes. This document focuses on the use of PIV Cards to gain access to federal buildings and facilities. It does not address non-PIV credentials that may be issued to populations that do not fall under the scope of HSPD-12 but require access to federal facilities.

Table of Contents

1. **Introduction** 1

1.1   Background 1

1.2   Purpose and Scope 1

2. **Characteristics of PIV Implementations** 3

2.1   Benefits of the Complete Implementation 3

2.2   Qualities of the Complete Implementation 4

2.3   Interoperability Qualities 5

2.4   Infrastructure Requirements 6

3. **Threat Environment** 7

3.1   Identifier Collisions 7

3.2   Revoked PIV Cards 8

3.3   Visual Counterfeiting 8

3.4   Skimming 9

3.5   Sniffing 9

3.6   Social Engineering 10

3.7   Electronic Cloning 10

3.8   Electronic Counterfeiting 10

3.9   Other Threats 11

4. **PIV Authentication Mechanisms in PACS Applications** 12

4.1   PIV Authentication Mechanisms 12

4.2   Authentication Factors 12

4.3   Selection of PIV Authentication Factors 14

4.4   Credential Validation 19

5. **PACS Use Cases** 21

5.1   Single-Tenant Facility 22

5.2   Federal Multi-Tenant Facility 22

5.3   Mixed-Multi-Tenant Facility 23

5.4   Single-Tenant Campus 24

        5.4.1   FSL I or II Campus 24

        5.4.2   FSL III Campus 25

        5.4.3   FSL IV or V Campus 25

5.5   Federal Multi-Tenant Campus 26

6.   Deployment Consideration 27

6.1   PIV Identifiers 27

6.2   PACS Registration...28

6.3   Role-Based Access Control 30

6.4   Disaster Response and Recovery Incidents 30

6.5   Temporary Badges...31

6.6   Lost PIV Card or Suspicion of Fraudulent Use 31

6.7   PACS and ICAM Infrastructure 32

Appendix A — An Overview of PIV Authentication Mechanisms 33

A.1   Authentication using PIV Visual Credentials (VIS)...................................33

A.2   Authentication using the Cardholder Unique Identifier (CHUID)...............33

A.3   Authentication with the Card Authentication Certificate (PKI-CAK) 33

A.4   Authentication with the Symmetric Card Authentication Key (SYM-CAK)...34

A.5   Unattended Authentication Using Off-Card Biometric Comparison (BIO)...34

A.6   Attended Authentication Using Off-Card Biometric Comparison (BIO-A) ...34

A.7   Authentication with the PIV Authentication Certificate (PKI-AUTH).........35

A.8   Authentication Using On-Card Biometric Comparison (OCC-AUTH).........35

A.9   (PKI-CAK | SYM-CAK) + BIO(-A) Authentication 35

Appendix B — Combinations of PIV Authentication Mechanisms in PACS 37

Appendix C — Improving Authentication Transaction Times 40

Appendix D — FASC-N Uniqueness... 42

D.1   Full FASC-N Comparison...42

D.2   FASC-N Identifier Comparison...44

D.3   Partial FASC-N Comparison 44

D.4   Isomorphic FASC-N Comparison 45

Appendix E — Limitations of Legacy Physical Access Control Systems 46

E.1   Cardholder Identification..46

E.2   Door Reader Interface 46

E.3   Authentication Capability...47

E.4   Wiring 47

E.5   Software Upgrades 47

E.6   Legacy PACS Cards and PIV Card Differences 48

Appendix F — References.. 49

Appendix G — Terminology.. **51**

Appendix H — Abbreviations and Acronyms **59**

Appendix I — Revision History... **61**

List of Figures

Figure 4-1: Innermost Use of PIV Authentication Mechanisms 16

Figure 4-2: Examples of Mapping PIV Authentication Mechanisms... 18

Figure 5-1: Single-Tenant Facility Example.. 22

Figure 5-2: Multi-Tenant Facility Example 23

Figure 5-3: FSL I or II Campus Example 24

Figure 5-4: FSL III Campus Example 25

Figure 5-5: FSL IV or V Campus Example... 25

List of Tables

Table 4-1 - PIV Authentication Mechanisms on the Contact Interface.. 13

Table 4-2 - PIV Authentication Mechanisms on the Contactless Interface................................. 14

Table 4-3 - Authentication Factors for Security Areas... 15

Table 6-1 - PIV Identifiers.. 27

1. Introduction

1.1 Background

Homeland Security Presidential Directive-12 [HSPD-12] mandated the establishment of a government-wide standard for identity credentials to improve physical security in federally-controlled facilities.[2] To that end, [HSPD-12] required government employees and contractors be issued a new identity credential based on [FIPS201], *Personal Identity Verification (PIV) for Federal Employees and Contractors,* in accordance with OMB and OPM guidance.[3] Following [FIPS201], this credential is referred to herein as the PIV Card.[4]

[HSPD-12] explicitly requires the use of PIV credentials "in gaining physical access to Federally-controlled facilities and logical access to Federally-controlled information systems." The PIV Card employs microprocessor-based smart card technology, and is designed to be counterfeit-resistant, tamper-resistant, and interoperable across Federal Government facilities. Additionally, the [FIPS201] standards suite defines the authentication mechanisms as transactions between a PIV Card and a relying party. [FIPS201] does not, however, elaborate on the uses and applications of the PIV Card. This document provides guidelines on the uses of PIV Cards with physical access control systems (PACS). This guideline is the first revision of the original version, and a list of changes from the initial guideline is provided in Appendix I, Revision History.

1.2 Purpose and Scope

The purpose of this document is to describe PIV-enabled PACSs that are government-wide interoperable. Specifically, the document recommends a risk-based approach for selecting appropriate PIV authentication mechanisms to manage physical access to Federal Government facilities and assets. With the intent to facilitate and encourage greater use of PIV Cards, this document:

+ Describes the implementation of PIV-enabled PACS.

+ Discusses the PIV Card capabilities so that a risk-based assessment can be aligned with the appropriate PIV authentication mechanism.

+ Outlines an overall strategy for PIV authentication mechanisms with agency facility PACS.

As stated above, this document focuses on the use of PIV Cards to gain access to federal buildings and facilities. It does not address non-PIV credentials that may be issued to populations that do not fall under the scope of HSPD-12 but require access to federal facilities.

Although the ergonomic design of PACS components is outside the scope of this publication, the 1998 Amendment to Section 508 of the Rehabilitation Act has special relevance to PACS

---

[2] Federally-controlled facilities as defined in Section 1D of OMB Memorandum M-05-24 [M-05-24].

[3] OMB Memorandum [M-05-24] and credentialing guidance issued the Office of Personnel Management (OPM) clarifies the eligibility requirements for a PIV Card.

[4] Federal agencies may refer to PIV Cards by other names, for example, "Common Access Cards (CAC)," "LincPass," "identity badges," or "access cards." In this document, all such credentials issued by an accredited PIV Card Issuer are called PIV Cards.

components [SECTION508]. PACS access controls are intended to be unavoidable. [SECTION508] should be considered early during projects that integrate the PIV System with PACS. [SECTION508] should be considered as it applies to enrollment software, smart card and biometric readers, monitoring systems, and access control point sensors and actuators.

Many other aspects of physical access control are outside the scope of this publication. Authorization (i.e., granting permission within a PACS for an identified person to pass access control points) is a critical security function, but is out of scope for the PIV System. Other out of scope functions include area protection, intrusion detection, egress, monitoring and tracking (other than at access control points), and enforcement of access control decisions. It is understood that PACS may also be integrated with surveillance systems, fire control systems, evacuation systems, etc., within a facility. This document does not address the integration of PACS with other facility-centric information technology (IT) systems, although it has been written to minimize conflicts during such integration. Therefore, if the integration of the measures outlined in this document creates a life-safety risk, organizations will need to mitigate these risks before applying the measures.

The evaluation of specific PACS architectures or implementations is also outside the scope of this publication, as is the standardization of PACS. Unless normatively referenced, this document is a best practice guideline.

> **Recommendation 1.1:** This document recommends a risk-based approach for selecting appropriate PIV authentication mechanisms to manage physical access to Federal Government facilities and assets. Agencies should seek recommendations on PACS architectures, authorization, and facility protection from other sources.

> **Recommendation 1.2:** Information systems security protections apply to PACSs as PACSs are considered IT systems. PACS information systems include, for example, servers, databases, workstations and network appliances in either shared or isolated networks.

2. Characteristics of PIV Implementations

[HSPD-12] directs federal departments and agencies to improve identification and authentication of federal employees and contractors requiring access to federally controlled facilities through the widespread application of [FIPS201], the Standard that was developed in response to [HSPD-12]. This standard defines the characteristics of the PIV System.

This section describes the main characteristics and qualities of a deployed PIV System that uses the PIV Card for electronic authentication of people for facility access managed by the United States Government. The [FIPS201] authentication mechanisms that can be performed electronically at facility access points are PKI-CAK, SYM-CAK, BIO, BIO-A, PKI-AUTH and OCC-AUTH.[5] The VIS authentication mechanism cannot be verified electronically and provides "LITTLE to NO" confidence in the identity of the cardholder. It should not be used when another mechanism is practical. Similarly, authentication mechanisms other than the CHUID authentication mechanisms must be implemented, since [FIPS201] deprecates the use of the CHUID authentication mechanism as it provides 'LITTLE or NO' confidence in the identity of the cardholder.[6] Newly purchased systems must support other authentication mechanisms (e.g., PKI-CAK) besides the CHUID mechanism.

2.1 Benefits of the Complete Implementation

The complete PIV System is an identity infrastructure that is attractive to federal agencies, application owners, and contractors because of these benefits:

+ Enhanced trust. PIV Cards are issued in accordance with standardized, audited processes, which exceeds the level for low- and moderate-impact legacy applications, and equals best practice reached for high-impact applications.

+ Resistance to misuse and cloning. Electronic validation of the PIV Card, using digital signatures, makes it tamper-resistant. Cryptographic challenge/response protocols make the PIV Card counterfeit-resistant. Biometric authentication makes the PIV Card non-transferable.

+ Status and revocation. PIV Card Issuer process assurance will extend beyond the issuance action to PIV Card validation and revocation services (see Section 4.4). These services are required elements of the PIV infrastructure, and will be implemented, monitored, and audited with the same care as the PIV issuance process.

+ Standard identity infrastructure. Application developers will assume, as a default, that registration and authentication will use a PIV Card identity, reducing

---

5 The PIV authentication mechanisms are also described in Appendix A.

[6] While use of the CHUID authentication mechanism has been deprecated, the on-card CHUID data element has not been deprecated and continues to be mandatory. In addition to being the only data element in which the optional Cardholder UUID appears, [FIPS201] permits the CHUID data element to be used in the BIO(-A) and SYM-CAK authentication mechanisms as a source for the card's expiration date and for a unique identifier from the PIV Card.

development cost, registration time, and the application learning curve for new subjects.

+ Integrated system. PACS will be fully integrated with other PIV system components that perform provisioning, enrollment, and finalization.

+ Fewer credentials. A single PIV Card provides a small set of authentication methods that are applicable to many applications and in many contexts. This means significantly fewer identity credentials that need to be issued and significantly fewer account enrollments.

Each of these points both enhances security and creates efficiency of operation. Reusing identity enrollment across multiple applications, collapsing redundant status and revocation processes (separate processes for revocation on termination across multiple applications), and replacing authentication credentials that are easily shared or transferred will reduce operating costs borne by federal agencies. Availability of a skilled workforce familiar with the standardized PIV identity infrastructure, implementation of PIV issuance with a standardized identity verification methodology, the existence of high-availability online services for PIV Card status and validation, and pre-enrollment in a graduated, multi-factor authentication scheme all enhance security current practice in many applications.

2.2   Qualities of the Complete Implementation

The PIV System implementation is complete when it exhibits the following qualities.

1. PIV authentication mechanisms are used wherever they are applicable, in accordance with [HSPD-12] and [FIPS201].

2. Electronic authentication (as opposed to VIS authentication) is the common practice.

3. Electronic validation of the PIV Card is done at or near the time of authentication (see Section 4.4).[7]

4. All PIV Card access control decisions are made by comparing the selected PIV identifier to access control list (ACL) entries. See Section 6.1 and Appendix D for details. PIV authentication mechanisms are applied based on the impact assessed for the area so that each facility is mapped to the "Controlled, Limited, Exclusion" model and an assignment of PIV authentication mechanisms to all access control points in accordance with Section 4.2.

5. Cryptographic and biometric authentications are applied widely in low, moderate, and high impact [FIPS199] areas.

6. Agencies exhibit reciprocal trust in the process assurance of PIV card issuers (PCIs).

---

[7] In some cases, validating PIV Cards at the time of authentication is not practical. In these instances, it is possible to maintain a local cache of validated PIV Cards, provided that the cache is updated regularly.

7. Both new and upgraded PACS applications accept PIV Cards as proof of identity for user authentication, and, where applicable, user registration/provisioning.

8. Authentication transactions have been optimized; especially at access points that only require one-factor authentication and that have high throughput requirements.

2.3   Interoperability Qualities

Interoperability for PIV-based facility access means the ability of a PACS to use any PIV Card issued by any agency to authenticate the cardholder by performing one or more PIV authentication mechanisms. In other words, the PACS has to support at least one PIV authentication mechanism that is supported by all PIV Cards.[8]

The interoperability goal of a PIV-enabled PACS can be stated:

1. Any PIV Card can provide verification of identity to the PACS (access is granted only if the identity is so authorized).

2. After a successful authentication, the authentication mechanism provides the cardholder's authenticated identity (see Section 6.1) to the relying party.

+ The PACS supports at least one PIV authentication mechanism that is supported by all PIV Cards. For example, a PACS may use the PKI-AUTH authentication mechanism to authenticate all cardholders. Alternatively, the PACS may use the BIO authentication mechanism to authenticate most cardholders but use the PKI-AUTH authentication mechanism to authenticate those cardholders from whom fingerprints could not be collected.

+ A relying PACS application needs to support all acceptable algorithms, key lengths, and key material that could be presented, either by a PIV Card or by the PIV infrastructure. For PIV Card, these data objects and keys are placed on a PIV Card during issuance and use specific cryptographic algorithms selected from the acceptable algorithms in [SP800-78], *Cryptographic Algorithms and Key Sizes for Personal Identity Verification*. The PACS application interrogates the card to learn which algorithms are used.

  o If the PKI-CAK authentication mechanism is performed by a PACS application, the PACS should support all of the asymmetric algorithms permitted for the asymmetric Card Authentication key, as specified in Table 3-1 of [SP800-78], i.e., RSA 2048 and ECDSA P-256, and the PACS should accept all valid Card Authentication certificates.

---

[8] Section 4.2 indicates which authentication mechanisms can be implemented using only data objects that are mandatory under FIPS 201-2. However, not all these authentication mechanisms are supported by all PIV Cards, as PKI-CAK is not supported by some cards issued under FIPS 201-1 and fingerprints cannot be collected from all cardholders.

- o If the PKI-AUTH authentication mechanism is performed by a PACS, the accepted algorithms will be the same as PKI-CAK, but the PACS will accept only PIV Authentication certificates and require PIN entry.

- o If authentication using off-card biometric comparison is performed (BIO or BIO-A), the PACS should support all of the signature algorithms and key sizes permitted by Table 3-2 of [SP800-78].

- o Signature verification and path validation is performed on all signed data objects for the PIV authentication mechanisms used. Failure of signature verification or path validation results in a failed authentication attempt that does not admit a cardholder for access. Caching of validation results (with periodic recheck) is preferred in certain circumstances (see Section 4.4).

- + PINs required for PIV authentication mechanisms are strings of six to eight decimal digits. For PKI-AUTH, BIO, and BIO-A authentication mechanisms, a PIN entry device must acquire the PIN from the cardholder and present it to the PIV Card for activation.

As per OMB policy, installed PACS readers are required to be from the approved products list of the General Services Administration (GSA) FIPS 201 Evaluation Program [FIPS 201 EP]. Each of these readers are capable of one or more PIV authentication mechanisms, such that each PACS reader can support the authentication of any PIV cardholder using a PIV authentication mechanism, including those with PIV Cards that do not implement any of the optional card capabilities. Note that in this document, a PACS reader's authentication capabilities is assumed to be supported by a PACS controller since the controller is usually the component to execute or support execution of the PIV authentication mechanisms, while the reader functions as the interface between the PIV Card and the controller.

The ability of a PIV Card and cardholder to authenticate at a reader does not mean they will be granted access—it means only that the cardholder's identity has been verified, with the assurance level of the authentication mechanism employed, by the reader. A cardholder must authenticate and be authorized to be granted access. Authorization policies and mechanisms are outside the scope of [FIPS201].

2.4   Infrastructure Requirements

The qualities and benefits of the complete PIV System can only be achieved if its implementation is supported by bi-directional communications infrastructure used in modern PACS. The following areas have significant influence on the rate at which the complete PIV System integration can be achieved by PACS, and should therefore be supported by PACS upgrades and new PACS procurements:

1. Fast network or two-way serial communication among PACS readers and controllers, panels and head-end components.

2. Fast network communication for PIV status and validation services.

Point (1) allows the PACS to quickly issue commands to cards and receive responses while Point (2) allows direct access to PIV status and validation services, if needed.

3.   Threat Environment

The PIV System is intended to enhance security and trust in identity credentials, but no practical system can guarantee perfect security. This section discusses known technical threats to PIV authentication mechanisms. The CHUID authentication mechanism especially is vulnerable to security threats as described in this section. For that reason, the authentication mechanism has been deprecated. Other authentication mechanisms other than the CHUID authentication mechanisms *(e.g., PKI-CAK)* must be implemented. Methods of attack are described in general terms, and this is not an exhaustive list of possible attacks. Attackers often succeed by exploiting overlooked or newly introduced vulnerabilities in operational systems.

The PIV System protects the trustworthiness of the PIV Card data objects through PIV Card access rules and digital signatures. Overall trust in the execution of a PIV authentication mechanism is also dependent on correct operation of the PIV Card, the PACS, and the PIV Card validation infrastructure, and, to a degree, on protecting the confidentiality, integrity, and availability of the communication channels among them. Attacks may, therefore, be directed against any of these components, with varying difficulty and potential impact.

The factors critical to sustained trust in the PIV System are:

+ The strength of cryptographic operations.

+ The protection of private and secret keys by system components.

+ The successful decryption and/or signature verification of data objects at expected times.

+ The continuous implementation of access rules by the PIV Card to protect access to the data and keys on the card.

+ The dependable operation of other system elements in the PIV System and the PACS.

To execute a PIV authentication mechanism, the cardholder presents his or her card to the PACS. The presentation of the PIV Card occurs outside the security perimeter to which access is requested. When the presentation occurs at the outermost perimeter of a facility, the cardholder is in an Unrestricted area, and various technical attacks on PACS are easily carried out. Special security precautions must be taken to ensure protection of these devices at the outermost perimeters of the facility. Even at interior perimeters, the degree of protection provided by enclosing perimeters may be modest when the means of attack can be easily concealed. Possible attack vectors include identifier collisions, revoked PIV Cards, visual counterfeiting, skimming, sniffing, social engineering, electronic cloning, and electronic counterfeiting. These methods of attack, as well as others, are discussed below.

3.1   Identifier Collisions

By definition, a unique identifier for a PIV Card is a data artifact with a fixed value unique to one particular PIV Card. PIV Card Issuers (PCIs) create unique identifiers during the card issuance process. The presence of unique identifiers allows a PIV Card to be uniquely identified by a relying system, such as a PACS. If the unique identifier is ever truncated, compressed, hashed, or modified, information could be lost. If information is lost from the unique identifier before it is compared against access control list (ACL) entries, multiple cards may generate the same reduced identifier. This is called an *identifier collision*. A collision means that multiple PIV Cards will appear to belong to the same person and will all be granted the same access privileges.

> *The PIV Card mitigates the risk of collision by defining a unique Federal Agency Smartcard Number (FASC-N) Identifier for the purposes of physical access control decisions. To prevent collisions, all access control decisions based on the FASC-N should be made by comparing the 14-decimal-digit FASC-N Identifier, and optionally the values of additional FASC-N fields, against the ACL entries. [FIPS201] added the mandatory card universally unique identifier (Card UUID), which is also a unique identifier that can be used reliably in access control decisions. See Section 6.1 for PIV identifiers.*

3.2 Revoked PIV Cards

PIV Cards may be revoked for a number of reasons, including a lost or stolen card. A revoked PIV Card could continue to open doors with the CHUID authentication mechanism long after the card has been revoked. As described in [FIPS201], the check for revocation should be performed by a status check, using either the Online Certificate Status Protocol (OCSP) or certificate revocation lists (CRL), on the PIV Authentication certificate or the Card Authentication certificate. Credential validation (see Section 4.4) is required by [FIPS201] for all PIV authentication mechanisms, however, validation of biometric and the CHUID credentials do not include a revocation check. If a PACS caches the status of PIV Cards, the cached status of a revoked PIV Card will remain "valid" until the cache is refreshed. The process for PACS de-authorization is not required or defined by [FIPS201], raising the possibility that online credential validation may not be implemented, or not effectively implemented, where the CHUID authentication mechanism is employed.

> *The PIV System mitigates the risk of use of a misappropriated PIV Card (which has been successfully reported and revoked) through the process of credential validation. Section 5.5 of [FIPS201] states that "the presence of a valid, unexpired, and unrevoked authentication certificate on a card is proof that the card was issued and is not revoked." In the CHUID authentication mechanism, only the CHUID data object is read from the PIV Card, and a reader cannot check the status of a PIV Authentication certificate on the basis of the CHUID alone. Therefore, it is recommended that path validation of the PIV Authentication certificate or the Card Authentication certificate be done at PIV registration, and periodically repeated by the PACS as long as registration is maintained. Implementation methods are further discussed in Section 6.2 and Section 4.4.*

3.3 Visual Counterfeiting

PIV Cards used in the VIS authentication mechanism are visually inspected by a security guard. A visual counterfeit mimics the appearance, but not the electronic behavior, of an actual PIV Card. A PIV replica may be created by color photocopying or graphic illustration methods and color printing to blank stock. Because of the required presence of one or more security features on the PIV Card, a visual counterfeit is unlikely to pass close examination, provided guards are trained to recognize security features. However, ID cards may receive only cursory examination when used as "flash passes."

The PIV Card mitigates the risk of visual counterfeiting through its capability for rapid electronic authentication, and to a lesser degree, by the presence of one or more security features on the surface of the card. Given the ready availability of high-quality scanners, graphic editing software, card stock, and smart card printers, electronic verification is strongly recommended, either in place of the VIS authentication mechanism or in combination with it. (Note that [FIPS201] downgraded the VIS Authentication mechanism to indicate that it provides "LITTLE or NO" confidence in the identity of the cardholder.)

3.4   Skimming

A contactless PIV Card reader with a sensitive antenna can be concealed in a briefcase, and is capable of reading [ISO/IEC 14443] contactless smart cards like the PIV Card at a distance of at least 25 cm, as demonstrated in [SKIMMER]. The range of a skimmer is limited primarily by the requirement for the skimmer to supply power to the PIV Card by inductive coupling. A concealed skimmer could immediately obtain the free-read data from the PIV Card through the contactless interface. [FIPS201] introduced the concept of an optional virtual contact interface (VCI), which allows all data on the PIV Card that is not protected by a PIN to be read once this interface is established. [SP 800-73], *Interfaces for Personal Identity Verification*, specifies an optional pairing code that can be used to authenticate the card reader to a PIV Card before the card establishes a VCI session. If agencies deploy PIV Cards that support establishing a VCI without requiring the submission of a pairing code, all data on these cards that is not protected by a PIN is vulnerable to skimming.

The PIV Card mitigates the risk of skimming by implementing access rules that prevent the release of biometric and other data over the contactless interface when a VCI has not been established, by requiring the use of a pairing code in order to establish a VCI. The risk of skimming can also be mitigated by employing shielding techniques that positively deactivate the PIV Card when not in use. The electromagnetically opaque holder mentioned in Section 2.11 of [FIPS201] is one such technique.

3.5   Sniffing

When a PIV Card is presented to a contactless reader at an access point, the reader supplies power to the PIV Card through inductive coupling and a series of messages is exchanged between the PIV Card and reader using radio frequency (RF) communications. A sniffer is a passive receiver that does not supply power to the smart card. A sniffer can operate at greater distance than a skimmer (sniffing at a distance of about 10 m has been reported), because a legitimate reader powers the PIV Card at the nominal distance of a few centimeters, while the sniffer's RF receiver is farther away. Potentially, a sniffer could capture the entire message transaction between the contactless reader and the PIV Card.

The PIV Card mitigates the risk of sniffing by the same access rules that prevent the release of biometric and other data over the contactless interface. The CHUID can be sniffed, however, when used over a contactless interface. Shielding techniques that positively deactivate a PIV Card when not in use cannot mitigate the risk of sniffing, because a PIV Card must be activated to perform a legitimate authentication transaction.

When a PIV Card that supports secure messaging[9] communicates with a contactless card reader, the card reader can leverage the secure channel, which would protect data objects being read from the risk of a sniffing attack.

3.6   Social Engineering

If an attacker persuaded the cardholder to give them possession of the PIV Card, the attacker could quickly copy all of the information that was not protected by the PIN. An attacker could also attempt a remote attack similar to well-known phishing attacks by creating a web page that asks the subject to "insert PIV Card and enter PIN" for an apparently legitimate purpose. If the cardholder complies, under some assumptions the attacker could capture the cardholder's PIN and all of the PIV data objects.

The PIV Card mitigates the risk of social engineering attacks by blocking the release of all private and secret keys, and by requiring two-factor authentication (PIV Card and PIN) to perform cryptographic operations with the PIV Authentication key. Moreover, the PIV Card is blocked upon exceeding the allocated number of bad PIN tries.

3.7   Electronic Cloning

If an attacker has successfully conducted a skimming, sniffing, or social engineering attack, he or she possesses verbatim copies of some of the data objects from an issued PIV Card. The objects that are signed (e.g., the certificates and CHUID) retain their signatures, and the signatures are valid if the original card is valid. The attacks described, however, cannot copy the private or secret keys needed for cryptographic authentication methods. The attacker is thus able to create a partial clone of the PIV Card that would succeed in a CHUID authentication but is not able to create a clone that would succeed in the PKI-CAK or PKI-AUTH authentication mechanisms.

The CHUID authentication mechanism has been deprecated. The PIV Card mitigates the risk of electronic cloning by providing alternative authentication mechanisms (e.g., PKI-CAK).

3.8   Electronic Counterfeiting

An attacker could construct a battery-powered, microprocessor-based device that emulates a PIV Card for purposes of the CHUID authentication mechanism. The attacker could program the microprocessor to generate and test CHUIDs repetitively against a PACS reader, changing the FASC-N credential identifier on each trial. This approach would not require prior capture of a valid CHUID, but since the counterfeit CHUIDs would not possess valid issuer signatures, a successful exploit depends on the absence of signature verification in the CHUID processing done by the reader.

The PIV Card mitigates the risk of electronic counterfeiting by storing a CHUID with a digital signature field. Electronic counterfeiting will be extremely difficult if CHUID

---

[9] Secure messaging is an optional mechanism specified in [SP 800-73] that provides confidentiality and integrity protection for the card commands that are sent to the card as well as for the responses received from the PIV Card.

signature verification is performed as required in [FIPS201].

3.9   Other Threats

The PIV and PACS systems are complex, and this brief discussion has focused on properties of the PIV Card. A number of other attack vectors have not been discussed in detail, including sophisticated technical attacks against the integrity of the PIV Card, PIV System, or PACS components, and cryptanalysis of the PIV cryptographic algorithms. While the impact of successful attacks such as these could be moderate to high, the probability of success is believed to be extremely low.

4. PIV Authentication Mechanisms in PACS Applications

This section provides a discussion of the application of the PIV authentication mechanisms in PACS environments. PIV authentication mechanisms offer a range of security measures (of different throughputs) that can be applied in a PACS environment. This section describes a measurement scale for authentication assurance relevant to PACS. It also provides recommendations on the use of PIV authentication mechanisms in a PACS environment. While a wide range of authentication mechanisms is identified, departments and agencies may adopt additional mechanisms that use the identity credentials on the PIV Card.

4.1 PIV Authentication Mechanisms

The [FIPS201] authentication mechanisms that can be performed electronically at facility access points are PKI-CAK, SYM-CAK, BIO, BIO-A, PKI-AUTH and OCC-AUTH. These mechanisms operate in several different ways as defined in [FIPS201], [SP800-73], and [SP800-76].[10] For example, a private key on the PIV Card may be used to sign a challenge (PKI-CAK and PKI-AUTH authentication mechanisms). A valid biometric from the card may be compared against a live scan (BIO, BIO-A, and OCC-AUTH authentication mechanisms).

> **Recommendation 4.1:** The VIS authentication mechanism cannot be verified electronically and provides "LITTLE to NO" confidence in the identity of the cardholder. It should not be used when another mechanism is practical.

> **Recommendation 4.2:** [FIPS201] deprecates the use of the CHUID authentication mechanism as it provides 'LITTLE or NO' confidence in the identity of the cardholder. Newly purchased systems must support other authentication mechanisms (e.g., PKI-CAK) in place of the CHUID authentication mechanism.

4.2 Authentication Factors

One of the functions of the PACS application is to verify the identity of the cardholder presenting a PIV Card. The PACS application may perform one or more authentication mechanisms using the PIV Card to establish confidence in the identity of the cardholder. The authentication of an identity is based on the verification of one, two, or three factors: a) "something you have," for example, possession of the PIV Card; b) "something you know," for example, knowledge of the PIN; and c) "something you are," for example, presentation of live fingerprints or irises by a cardholder.

The confidence in the cardholder's identity increases with the number of factors used to authenticate the PIV Card. Table 4-1 and Table 4-2 provide lists of PIV authentication mechanisms and their authentication factors when used on the contact and contactless interfaces, respectively. Many different combinations of the PIV authentication mechanisms are possible and an exhaustive list of combinations is provided in Appendix B.

Note that an authentication mechanism is not considered to provide any factors of authentication

---

[10] The PIV authentication mechanisms are also described in Appendix A.

if the authentication is not successful. For example, in the case of the PKI-AUTH and PKI-CAK authentication mechanisms, if the PACS application is unable to validate the authentication certificate from the presented card or does not receive a response to its challenge that can be verified using the public key in the certificate, then the PACS application cannot count the authentication attempt towards meeting the requirements for granting access to an area.

As noted in Section 2.3, in order to achieve interoperability, each access point in a PACS needs to support at least one PIV authentication mechanism that is supported by all PIV Cards.[11] In Table 4-1 and Table 4-2, the authentication mechanisms represented in **bold** are the authentication mechanisms that can be implemented using only features that are mandatory for PIV Cards issued under FIPS 201-2. Of these authentication mechanisms, however, only PKI-AUTH (when used in conjunction with the PIV Card PIN) and CHUID + VIS are currently supported by all PIV Cards. PKI-CAK is supported by all valid PIV Cards once all PIV Cards (issued under FIPS 201-1) without Card Authentication certificates have expired.

While the Cardholder Fingerprints data object needed for the BIO and BIO-A authentication mechanisms is mandatory, it may not be possible to collect usable fingerprints from some cardholders. So, PACS that use BIO(-A) to authenticate cardholders should be prepared to use an alternative authentication mechanism with PIV Cards that have no minutiae in the Cardholder Fingerprints data object (see Section 4.4.3 of [SP800-76]). PKI-AUTH is the recommended alternate authentication mechanism.

Table 4-1 - PIV Authentication Mechanisms on the Contact Interface

PIV Authentication Mechanism	Have	Know	Are	Authentication Factors
CHUIDdeprecated **+ VIS**	x			1
BIO			x	1
SYM-CAK	x			1
PKI-CAK	x			1
BIO-A	x		x	2
PKI-AUTH (with PIN)	x	x**		2
PKI-AUTH (with OCC)	x		x***	2
OCC-AUTH	x		x	2
SYM-CAK + BIO(-A)	x	x	x	3
PKI-CAK + BIO(-A)	x	x	x	3

Table 4-2 provides a list of PIV Authentication mechanisms that are appropriate for use over the

---

[11] Access points that need to perform three-factor authentication will need to support at least two authentication mechanisms.

** If the PIN is used to satisfy the security condition for use, then the PKI-AUTH authentication mechanism provides the following 2 factors of authentication: (i) something you have (i.e., the card) and (ii) something you know (i.e., the PIN).

*** If OCC is used to satisfy the security condition for use, then the PKI-AUTH authentication mechanism provides the following 2 factors of authentication: (i) something you have (i.e., the card) and (ii) something you are (i.e., on-card biometric match). Note that OCC is an optional PIV Card feature. As result, PKI-AUTH does not support interagency interoperability when OCC is used to satisfy the security condition of use. Use of the PIV Card PIN, on the other hand, enables the PKI-AUTH authentication mechanism to achieve interagency interoperability.

contactless interface. Note that there are some authentication mechanisms listed in Table 4-1 for use over the contact interface that are not listed in Table 4-2. The authentication mechanisms that are not listed in Table 4-2 are authentication mechanisms that would require the use of secure messaging when performed over the contactless interface, but that do not require the use of secure messaging when performed over the contact interface. Since support for secure messaging is optional, these authentication mechanisms do not support interagency interoperability when performed over the contactless interface, but (with the exception of SYM-CAK + BIO(-A)) do support interagency interoperability when performed over the contact interface, and so use of the contact interface is preferable for these authentication mechanisms.

Table 4-2 - PIV Authentication Mechanisms on the Contactless Interface

PIV Authentication Mechanism	Have	Know	Are	Authentication Factors
CHUID[deprecated] + VIS	x			1
SYM-CAK	x			1
PKI-CAK	x			1
OCC-AUTH	x		x	2

4.3   Selection of PIV Authentication Factors

A risk-based approach should be used when selecting appropriate PIV authentication mechanisms for physical access to Federal Government buildings and facilities, regardless of whether they are leased or government-owned. Determining risk to the facility is beyond the scope of this document; however, an agency may use a Facility Security Level (FSL) Determination[12] to derive the FSL for its facilities. There is no simple one-to-one mapping between the FSL and the authentication mechanism(s) that should be employed. An FSL I campus facility may have a need for nested perimeters due to localized high-value assets. An FSL III facility may not have any high-value assets but may be larger in population. An FSL V facility may need the highest level of authentication assurance at all access points except the public entrance to a visitor center.

For these reasons, it is recommended that authentication mechanisms be selected on the basis of protective areas established around assets or resources. This document adopts the concept of "Controlled, Limited, Exclusion" areas. Procedurally, proof of affiliation is often sufficient to gain access to a Controlled area (e.g., all employees and contractors of an agency are authorized to access that agency's headquarters' outer perimeter). Access to Limited areas is often based on functional subgroups or roles (e.g., all employees and contractors of a division are authorized to access that division's building or wing). The individual membership in the group or privilege of the role is established by authentication of the identity of the cardholder. Access to Exclusion areas may be gained by individual authorization only. Federal Government facilities can be identified and categorized in these areas and correspond generally to LOW (for Controlled), MODERATE (for Limited), and HIGH (for Exclusion) impact assets or resources [FIPS199]. This document recommends that Table 4-3 be used to determine the minimum number of

---

[12] FSL determination is the criteria and process used in determining the security level of a Federal facility, as described in "The Risk Management Process for Federal Facilities: An Interagency Security Committee Standard" [ISC-RMP].

authentication factors needed to satisfy security requirements of the area.[13]

Table 4-3 - Authentication Factors for Security Areas

Security Areas	Minimum Number of Authentication Factors Required
Controlled	1
Limited	2
Exclusion	3

If protective areas are nested, then authentication in context may be leveraged in obtaining the minimum number of authentication factors required for an area. For example, if a Limited area can only be accessed from a Controlled area, and PKI-CAK authentication is required to access the Controlled area, then BIO authentication may be used as the authentication mechanism for determining access to the Limited area, as two different factors of authentication (something you have and something you are) are authenticated before access to the Limited area is granted. Similarly, if an Exclusion area can only be accessed from a Limited area, and BIO authentication is required to access the Limited area, then PKI-AUTH (with PIN) authentication may be used as the authentication mechanism for determining access to the Exclusion area.

Authentication in context may be leveraged only when protections are in place to reduce the risks of piggybacking and tailgating, to ensure that the cardholder authenticated at the outer perimeter prior to the inner perimeter. This may be done by using gates or turnstiles at access points that physically prevent more than one person from passing through an access point after each authentication. Authentication in context may also be leveraged if the PACS can store and recall recent access control decisions and will only grant access through an inner perimeter if the individual recently authenticated at the outer perimeter.[14]

Figure 4-1 illustrates the innermost perimeter at which each PIV authentication mechanism may be used based on the authentication assurance level of the mechanism. Table 4-3 and Figure 4-1 both express constraints on the authentication mechanism that may be selected. The combined effect of Table 4-3 and Figure 4-1 determines exactly what mechanisms may be used. An exhaustive list of possible uses of PIV authentication mechanisms within protected areas is provided in Appendix B.

---

[13] As noted in Section 4.2, the security requirements of an area may only be satisfied by authentication mechanisms that are performed successfully (e.g., all signatures can be verified and all certificates are currently valid (not expired or revoked)).

[14] An authentication to an outer perimeter would be considered "recent" if it is reasonable to believe that the individual has not left the protective area since the authentication was performed.

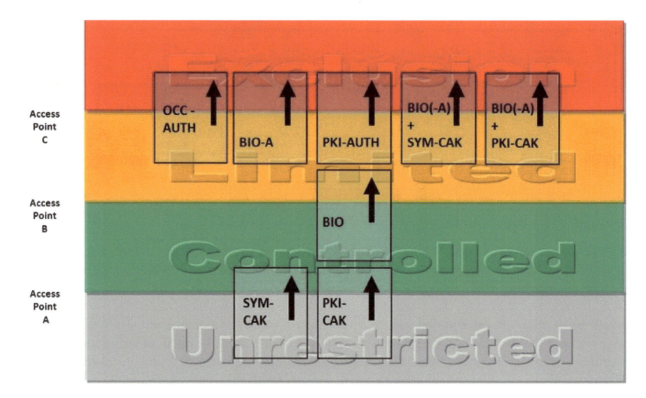

Figure 4-1: Innermost Use of PIV Authentication Mechanisms

The figure should be interpreted with the following notes:

Note 1. "BIO(-A) + PKI-CAK" means a combined authentication mechanism performing PKI-CAK and BIO or PKI-CAK and BIO-A at the same access point, both using the contact interface of the PIV Card. The term "combine" means that more than one independent authentication mechanism must successfully authenticate the presenting person, at the same access point, before access is permitted.

Note 2. Authentication mechanisms shown at a perimeter in Figure 4-1 may also be used alone at a perimeter farther out, subject to the requirements in Table 4-3, but not the reverse. If authentication mechanisms are combined in ways not shown in Figure 4-1, at least one of the combined mechanisms must be allowed by Figure 4-1 at the security perimeter of use.

Note 3. In a particular facility, a single perimeter may separate areas with a difference of more than one impact level. A single perimeter may allow access from Unrestricted to Limited, Unrestricted to Exclusion, or Controlled to Exclusion areas, and in these cases, the PIV authentication mechanisms should be combined to achieve necessary authentication factors to enter the innermost area.

Note 4. Within a Controlled or Limited area, an access point to an adjacent area at the same impact level may employ any of the authentication mechanisms shown in Figure 4-1.

Note 5. Within an Exclusion area, an access point to an adjacent area at the same impact level should use two or three-factor authentication.

Note 6.   In most cases, Figure 4-1 and these notes allow flexibility in the selection of specific authentication mechanisms. A decision should be made based on the local security policy and operational considerations.

Notes (3) and (5) ensure that two-factor authentication is always employed to enter Limited areas, and three-factor authentication is employed to enter Exclusion areas. It also ensures that credential validation is done in either case.

Notes (4) and (5) add some flexibility in the case of discretionary access control among areas at the same impact level.

The previous version of this document included the combined VIS + CHUID authentication mechanism as an option to transitioning from Unrestricted to Controlled areas. VIS + CHUID, however, is not included in this version of the document since both VIS and CHUID provide "LITTLE or NO" confidence in the identity of the cardholder. Other authentication mechanisms other than the CHUID authentication mechanisms must be implemented. Newly purchased systems must support other authentication mechanisms (e.g., PKI-CAK) besides the CHUID mechanism.

PIV authentication mechanisms can be mapped to perimeter crossings in many ways, provided that the requirements of this section are met. Figure 4-2 below provides some examples of mapping PIV authentication mechanisms to the perimeter crossings within a facility.

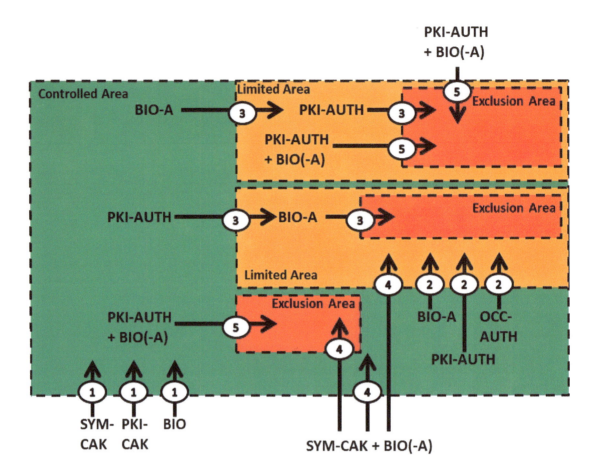

Figure 4-2: Examples of Mapping PIV Authentication Mechanisms

Figure 4-2 illustrates five different examples. Other sequences of authentication mechanisms are possible. Refer to Appendix B for a complete list of possible combinations of PIV authentication mechanisms that could be used in federal agency facility environments. Each example below is labeled with a number and is described as follows:

1. The PKI-CAK, SYM-CAK and BIO authentication mechanisms provide one-factor authentication and can be used to cross from Unrestricted to Controlled areas.

2. The BIO-A, PKI-AUTH and OCC-AUTH authentication mechanisms provide two-factor authentication and can be used to cross into Limited areas. The example shows these authentication mechanisms to cross from Controlled to Limited areas.

3. Authentication in context can be leveraged if the "Controlled, Limited, Exclusion" areas are nested. This example shows that if the BIO(-A) authentication mechanism is used to access the Limited area, then the PKI-AUTH authentication mechanism may be used to control access to the Exclusion area without requiring the cardholder to repeat the BIO(-A) authentication mechanism. Conversely, if the PKI-AUTH authentication mechanism was used to access the Limited area, then BIO-A authentication may be used to control access to the Exclusion area.

4. This example shows that an authentication at one level may be used at lower levels. This example shows the SYM-CAK + BIO(-A) authentication mechanism may be used to cross from Unrestricted to Controlled, Unrestricted to Limited, or Unrestricted to Exclusion.

5. This example shows that authentication in context is not always possible. The example shows that combined PKI-AUTH + BIO(-A) authentication mechanism may be used to cross from Unrestricted to Exclusion, Controlled to Exclusion, or Limited to Exclusion. Note that the three-factor authentication rule is observed in all possible crossings.

Figure 4-2 shows some legitimate examples of mapping PIV authentication mechanisms to the perimeter crossings. There are also authentication mechanisms that do not meet the requirements of Table 4-3. For example, the PKI-CAK or SYM-CAK authentication mechanism should not be used to access Limited or Exclusion areas. Limited and Exclusion areas require either two or three-factor authentication, while the PKI-CAK and SYM-CAK mechanisms only provide one-factor authentication. Also, sometimes combining authentication mechanisms does not add up to the required authentication factors. For example, PKI-CAK + PKI-AUTH is not a valid authentication mechanism to access Exclusion areas. Note that PKI-CAK + PKI-AUTH only provides two factors ("something you have" and "something you know") of authentication.

> **Recommendation 4.3:** Authentication assurance will be increased if a PACS uses relevant information from previous access control decisions ("context") when making a new access control decision. For example, if a cardholder attempts to pass from a Controlled to a Limited area, the PACS could require that the cardholder was recently allowed access to the Controlled area. Historically, rigorous implementation of this concept required person-traps and exit tracking, but partial implementations have significant value, and could be strengthened by new technology and systems integration.

4.4 Credential Validation

Credential validation is the process of determining if a presented identity credential is valid, i.e., was legitimately issued and has not expired or been revoked.

[FIPS201] requires that any credential used in an authentication mechanism be checked to ensure that it was legitimately issued. However, not all credentials on the PIV Card include an expiration date. So, when performing the BIO, BIO-A, OCC-AUTH or SYM-CAK authentication mechanism, an additional credential needs to be checked in order to verify that the PIV Card has not expired or been revoked. This additional credential may be the CHUID, the PIV Authentication certificate, or the Card Authentication certificate. When two or more credentials are used in an authentication mechanism, the credentials need to be checked to ensure they all came from the same card, by verifying that the same unique identifier (FASC-N or Card UUID) appears in all of them.

Particularly in the case of the authentication certificates, online credential validation is extremely valuable to relying parties because it retrieves the most up-to-date credential status, that block access of fraudulent PIV Cards that have been lost or stolen. However, online, on-demand credential validation may not always be practical. Some reasons include: (i) a noticeable delay in response time and (ii) absence of network connectivity to the certification authority. In these circumstances, it may be possible for PIV Cards of interest to be registered with a caching status proxy. The caching status proxy polls the status of all registered cards periodically and caches the status responses from their issuer(s). Relying parties will see quick query-response service from the caching status proxy. The cache status should be updated at least once every 24 hours.

> **Recommendation 4.4:** Online credential validation should be implemented for all of the PIV authentication mechanisms whenever most up-to-date status is necessary.

> **Recommendation 4.5:** Caching techniques should be used to implement credential validation for improved performance or when online, on-demand credential validation is not possible. It is also recommended that the cached data be protected against tampering.

> **Recommendation 4.6**: Credential status checks that indicate that the certificate has been revoked should always prevent a cardholder from access.

Data objects read from the PIV Card by a reader must not be fully trusted as authentic (i.e., produced by a PCI) and unmodified until their digital signatures are verified. Most data objects in a PIV Card Application have embedded digital signatures (i.e., all certificates, the CHUID, fingerprint templates, facial image, iris images, and security object). The authenticity of data objects that do not have embedded digital signatures (e.g., Card Capability Container (CCC), Discovery Object, Pairing Code, Printed Information Buffer) can be verified since hashes of these data objects are included in the Security Object.

Path validation (or *trust path validation*) is the process of verifying the binding between the subject identifier and subject public key in a certificate, based on the public key of a trust anchor, through the validation of a chain of certificates that begins with a certificate issued by the trust anchor and ends with the target certificate. The public key of a trust anchor is implicitly trusted by the relying party (generally, this means it was installed into the relying system by means of a trusted process, such as a direct device-to-device copy). Full trust in a PIV authentication mechanism requires that path validation succeed for each PIV data object used by the authentication mechanism.

[FIPS201] requires that path validation be performed for all PIV authentication mechanisms, since these authentication mechanisms can be fully trusted only if path validation is performed. In the absence of path validation, an impostor could forge a fingerprint template and a CHUID object, for example, with signatures from a phony certification authority. BIO authentication would succeed with this counterfeit PIV Card, and the forgery would not be detected.

> **Recommendation 4.7:** Credential validation must be performed on all signed data objects required by the authentication mechanism in use. Path validation of a certificate should employ either online or cached status checks depending on the authentication use case, the PACS environment and the performance requirements. Because path validation is a part of credential validation, both services can be economically implemented by a single PACS service component.

5. PACS Use Cases

[HSPD-12] requires that PIV credentials include graduated criteria, from least secure to most secure, for authentication to ensure flexibility in selecting the appropriate level of security for each application. PIV credentials, as defined in [FIPS201], offer a range of security, which is discussed in Section 4 and Appendix A. This section provides recommendations for the appropriate use of graduated security in PIV credentials for the PACS.

PIV credentials can be used at federally-owned buildings or leased spaces, single or multi-tenant occupancy, commercial spaces shared with non-government tenants, and government-owned contractor-operated facilities. This includes existing and new construction or major modernizations, standalone facilities, and federal campuses. Thus, PIV credentials apply to facilities requiring varying levels of security with differing security requirements.

To begin, the agency must know the security requirements for its facility and what assets they need to protect. Since this is beyond the scope of this document, it is assumed that the agency has completed its facility security risk assessment. It is also assumed that the agency is using the FSL determination [ISC-RMP] to derive the security requirement for its facility. The FSL takes into account size and population, as well as several other factors that capture the value of the facility to the government and to potential adversaries. Other factors, including mission criticality, symbolism, and threat to tenant agency, are also considered. For the purposes of protecting assets and placement of proper security measures, size and population may not be as important as the mission criticality, symbolism, and threat to the tenant agency. Although there is no simple one-to-one mapping between FSL and the authentication mechanism(s), the FSL indicates the general risk to the facility. Based on the FSL, an agency should identify and categorize PACS perimeters as protecting Controlled, Limited, or Exclusion areas. Appropriate security measures can then be implemented based on the areas identified in consultation with the real property authority and legal authority. This section provides example use cases of PIV authentication mechanisms in the following environments:

+ Single-Tenant Facility—A facility that only includes a federal tenant, or multiple components of the same department or agency that fall under one "umbrella" for security purposes.

+ Federal Multi-Tenant Facility—A facility that includes tenants from multiple federal departments and agencies, but no non-federal tenants.

+ Mixed-Multi-Tenant Facility—A facility that includes tenants from multiple federal departments and agencies as well as one or more non-federal tenants.

+ Single-Tenant Campus—Federal facilities with two or more buildings surrounded (and thus defined) by a perimeter.

+ Federal Multi-Tenant Campus—Two or more federal facilities located contiguous to one another and typically sharing some aspects of the environment, such as parking, courtyards, private vehicle access roads or gates, entrances to connected facilities, etc. May also be referred to as a "Federal center" or "Complex."

5.1   Single-Tenant Facility

In single-tenant facilities, a single tenant defines its own security requirements and controls its own security measures, which may require consultation with the real property authority as applicable. The facility may be an owned or a leased space. If the space is leased, the tenant usually can impose security requirements based on its needs defined in the lease. This type of facility may range from FSL I to FSL V. Therefore, it may have LOW, MODERATE, or HIGH value assets to protect. Facilities evaluated at FSL I or II may decline to implement PACS. Facilities evaluated at FSL III or above should implement PACS. These facilities may have general access areas where individual identification and authentication is not possible, or necessary. In this case, the agency should establish at least one perimeter beyond which individual authentication is required and conducted with PACS. Figure 5-1 is an example of a single-tenant facility with two security perimeters. The figure shows a building with multiple floors occupied by one tenant. One security perimeter is the lobby and the other is the entrance to a room that contains high-value assets (e.g., a server room). The two areas should each be designated as a Controlled, Limited, or Exclusion and the appropriate authentication mechanisms should be selected from Table 4-1 or Table 4-2 for each perimeter.

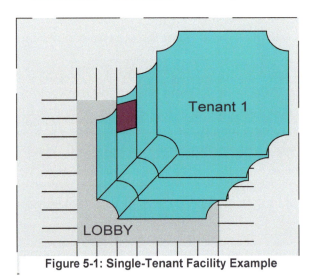

Figure 5-1: Single-Tenant Facility Example

5.2   Federal Multi-Tenant Facility

The challenge with a multi-tenant facility is to meet the security policies and requirements of the individual tenants in the facility. Some tenants may need higher security than others. The security policies may not be uniform and cannot be imposed upon others. In this situation, a determination has to be made by the Facility Security Committee, the owning or leasing department or agency, and the security organization responsible for the facility to identify appropriate areas within the facility. In the end, the decision may be to implement the highest necessary security for the entire facility or to apply the lowest security to the facility while affording individual agencies additional security at their interior perimeters.

If the highest security is implemented for the entire facility, there is one security perimeter. Otherwise, the multi-tenant facility may be viewed as an outer and inner perimeter where different security can be implemented. The outer perimeter is the most common security measure that all the tenants agreed to and the inner perimeter is an agency-specific security measure. For example, the facility may designate Controlled area at the outer perimeter but one of the tenant agencies may require Exclusion area protection for their inner area. Access to the building may be generally satisfied with a Controlled area authentication mechanism, but the individual agency should implement an Exclusion area authentication mechanism for access to its spaces(s). In this example, the building is the outer perimeter while access to an individual floor is the inner perimeter.

Since there are multiple tenants in the facility, it is strongly recommended that each individual tenant designate its own "Controlled, Limited, Exclusion" areas and employ appropriate [FIPS201] authentication mechanisms as in Figure 4-1. Since by definition the multi-tenant facility hosts Federal Government employees and contractors, the outer perimeter can be PIV-enabled and individual agencies may piggyback on the authentication performed at the outer perimeter. Figure 5-2 is an example of a multi-tenant facility. The building lobby is the outer perimeter implementing PIV-enabled PACS, while the individual tenants implement additional security perimeters for stronger cardholder authentication.

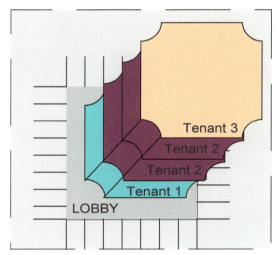

Figure 5-2: Multi-Tenant Facility Example

5.3   Mixed-Multi-Tenant Facility

The mixed-multi-tenant facility use case is an example of a facility with a mix of PIV cardholders and non-PIV cardholders. Therefore, some tenants in this facility may not possess PIV Cards for authentication. It may be difficult if not impossible to develop one acceptable security policy for all the tenants. The federal tenants in this facility should ensure they have leverage to implement necessary PIV authentication mechanisms for access to their space. The tenant agencies should designate their own "Controlled, Limited, Exclusion" areas and then evaluate if the facility's PACS will accommodate their security needs. Each Federal Government tenant should ensure an appropriate PIV authentication mechanism from Table 4-1 or Table 4-2 is implemented for its designated areas. If the facility's PACS cannot accommodate agencies' security needs, the tenant agencies should establish their own PACS. This may be considered an inner perimeter to the facility. In this case, the outer perimeter (i.e., access to the building) does not provide any authentication context. The individual agency should manage its own PACS server and user access.

5.4   Single-Tenant Campus

A campus is a collection of buildings, labs, and parking spaces that are geographically co-located within a large perimeter. The large perimeter is typically a fenced compound with a gate through which federal employees, contractors, and visitors gain access. A single-tenant campus may be assessed at FSL III or above simply due to its population and size. All the areas within the campus may not have the same security requirements. Some spaces may be generally accessible to campus visitors, while some may be specialized spaces such as a high-security lab or a chemical storage area that require a higher level of security protection. In this scenario, one security measure for all spaces might be overbearing and hamper business processes. The campus environment can be further characterized as one big perimeter (outer perimeter) and multiple smaller (inner) perimeters. There are interdependencies between these perimeters that are further elaborated through the "Controlled, Limited, Exclusion" areas.

In the campus environment, a cumulative effect of authentication is achieved as an individual traverses boundaries from Unrestricted to Controlled to Limited to Exclusion areas. In other words, authentication performed to gain access to a Controlled area should not be repeated to gain access to a Limited area. Instead, a complementary evidence of identity should be used to achieve multi-factor authentication of the individual who requests access to the Limited area. The same logic applies to the Exclusion area.

Spaces within a campus may have varying degrees of security. The campus may be subdivided into "Controlled, Limited, Exclusion" areas. A single Controlled or Limited area may be divided into sub-areas for purposes of discretionary or need-to-know access control. As a matter of local policy, the use of single-factor authentication may be sufficient to access sub-areas within the same Controlled or Limited area.

The following sections discuss the use of PIV authentication mechanisms in a campus environment with multiple perimeters. This document does not address non-PIV authentication mechanisms.

5.4.1   FSL I or II Campus

Figure 5-3 depicts a security posture of an FSL I or II campus. It includes one or more Controlled areas that are available to authorized personnel. Since an FSL I or II campus can be considered a low-risk area, a PACS may or may not be maintained to preclude unauthorized entries. When PACS is maintained, SOME confidence in the identity of the cardholder should be achieved. Implementation of PIV authentication mechanisms for Controlled areas would be an appropriate countermeasure for security. PKI-CAK, SYM-CAK, and BIO are the three recommended authentication mechanisms in this environment. Note that these authentication mechanisms validate "something you have" or "something you are" (one-factor authentication).

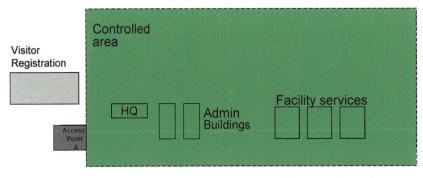

Figure 5-3: FSL I or II Campus Example

5.4.2   FSL III Campus

Figure 5-4 depicts a security posture of an FSL III campus. It includes one or more Controlled areas as well as Limited areas that are restricted to specific groups of individuals. Since an FSL III campus can be considered moderate-risk, a PACS should provide additional security to the more valuable assets. HIGH confidence in the identity of the cardholder should be achieved for access to the Limited area. Note that the entire campus does not need the highest level of security. Implementation of BIO(-A), PKI-AUTH or OCC-AUTH authentication mechanisms would be an appropriate countermeasure for the Limited area.[15]

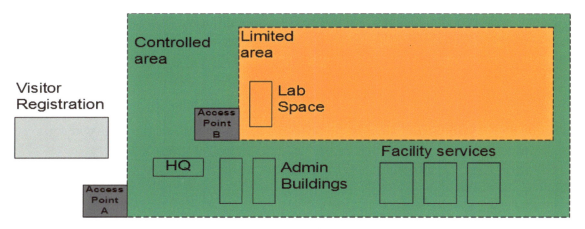

Figure 5-4: FSL III Campus Example

5.4.3   FSL IV or V Campus

Figure 5-5 depicts a security posture of an FSL IV or V campus. It includes one or more Controlled areas, Limited areas, and Exclusion areas that are restricted to specific groups of individuals.

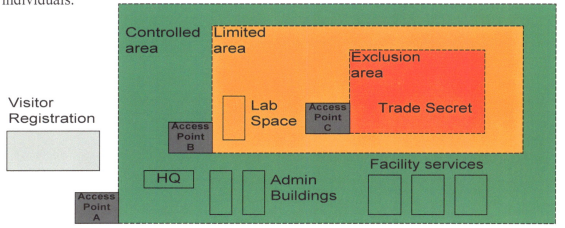

Figure 5-5: FSL IV or V Campus Example

Although there is not a simple one-to-one mapping between FSLs and PACS authentication

---

[15] Use of the BIO authentication mechanism for access to the Limited area would require the ability to use authentication in context where it is known that the cardholder needed to perform the PKI-CAK, SYM-CAK, BIO-A, PKI-AUTH, or OCC-AUTH authentication mechanism in order to access the Controlled area.

assurance levels at access control points, generally higher-risk areas will need stronger identity assurance. Since an FSL IV or V campus is considered a high-risk area, a PACS should achieve VERY HIGH confidence in the identity of the cardholder for access to the Exclusion areas. Note that the entire campus does not need the highest level of confidence in the identity of the cardholder. For access to the Exclusion areas, three-factor authentication should be achieved. This can be accomplished in multiple ways, as shown in Figure 4-2.

5.5   Federal Multi-Tenant Campus

The multi-tenant campus is similar to the single-tenant campus except that individual tenants will have their own security policies and the enforcement may be different. A tenant may benefit from the authentication mechanism(s) implemented at the outer perimeter; however, agencies may implement their own PACS within their space. In this case, if an agency were to benefit from other agencies' PACS, its PACS should have communication links with other PACS on the campus.

Each individual tenant within a campus should designate its own Controlled, Limited and Exclusion areas and identify appropriate PIV authentication mechanisms required for access to its space (see Figure 4-1). The tenants can then determine if they can simply use the campus PACS application, if they should add security by implementing an additional PIV authentication mechanism, or if they should implement a stand-alone PACS. Each individual tenant should ensure that appropriate PIV authentication mechanisms from Figure 4-1 are implemented for its designated areas.

6. Deployment Consideration

This section covers additional aspects and use cases that a PACS should take into consideration for a PIV-in-PACS System.

6.1 PIV Identifiers

The final step in each of the electronic authentication mechanisms described in [FIPS201] is that a unique identifier from one of the data objects that has been validated is used as input to an access control decision. Access control decisions can be made by comparing a unique identifier from the card (a PIV identifier) against access control list (ACL) entries. Examples of PIV identifiers used in access control decisions include the FASC-N (entire or part of), the Card Universally Unique Identifier (UUID), and the optional Cardholder UUID. So, a PACS may, for example, perform the PKI-CAK authentication mechanism, and then, if the authentication is successful, extract the FASC-N from the validated Card Authentication certificate and grant the cardholder access if the FASC-N appears on the ACL.

When deciding on the identifier to be used for access control decisions, agencies should consider the advantages and disadvantages of each type. Some of these decisions include the need to be able to grant access to holders of PIV Cards issued by another agency, and whether the agency will grant access to holders of PIV-Interoperable Cards (PIV-I Cards[16]).

Table 6-1 illustrates the pros and cons of using each identifier:

Table 6-1 - PIV Identifiers

PIV Identifier	Pros	Cons
FASC-N	• Available on all PIV Cards • Access control permissions can be based on one or more fields within the FASC-N	• ACL entries may need to change every time a PIV Card is re-issued. (See Appendix D) • May not be available on PIV-I Cards
Card UUID	• Available on all PIV-I Cards • Available on all PIV Card issued under FIPS 201-2	• ACL entries have to be updated every time a PIV or PIV-I Card is re-issued • May not be available on PIV Cards issued under FIPS 201-1
Cardholder UUID	• ACL entries do not have to be updated every time a cardholder is issued a new card	• Not available on all cards since it is optional • Only appears in the CHUID data object[17]

---

[16] PIV-I Cards are identity cards that are issued in a manner that allows federal relying parties to trust the cards and that meet the technical standards to work with PIV infrastructure elements such as card readers, but that do not meet all the requirements of [FIPS201]. PIV-I Cards are defined in [PIV-I].

[17] While use of the CHUID authentication mechanism has been deprecated, the on-card CHUID data element has not been

The FASC-N is a required data element on the PIV Card, which enables agencies to use it as an identifier for access control decisions. An advantage of the FASC-N over the Card UUID and the Cardholder UUID is that ACLs can be based on one or more fields within the FASC-N (see Appendix D). The FASC-Ns on PIV-I Cards, however, cannot always be used in access control decisions, since they may not be assigned in a manner that ensure uniqueness.[18]

The Card UUID is a required data element for PIV-I Cards that enables departments and agencies to identify a PIV-I cardholder. The Card UUID is also a required data element for PIV Cards issued under FIPS 201-2 PACS will be able to use the Card UUID in ACLs with all FIPS 201-2 PIV and PIV-I Cards.

The Cardholder UUID is an optional data element introduced in FIPS 201-2. Unlike the FASC-N and Card UUID, the Cardholder UUID is a persistent identifier for the cardholder that does not change when the cardholder receives a replacement card. So, for cards that have a Cardholder UUID, use of the Cardholder UUID can avoid the need to update ACL entries every time a cardholder is issued a new card. However, since the Cardholder UUID only appears in the CHUID data object, use of this identifier to make access control decisions would tend to increase transaction times, as there would be a requirement to authenticate the cardholder (e.g., using PKI-CAK), then read and validate the CHUID data object, and then compare an identifier in the CHUID data object to an identifier in the data object used during the authentication in order to ensure that both data objects were issued to the same card (e.g., comparing the Card UUID in the CHUID to the Card UUID in the Card Authentication certificate). An alternative would be to store both the Cardholder UUID and either the FASC-N or Card UUID in the ACL, grant access if the card's FASC-N or Card UUID is present on the ACL, and only check the Cardholder UUID if the presented FASC-N or Card UUID is not on the ACL. If the Cardholder UUID is found on the ACL, then the corresponding FASC-N or Card UUID should be updated in the ACL for use in future transactions.

6.2   PACS Registration

Before a PACS may grant access to a cardholder, the cardholder must be authorized for access in the PACS. Authorization may be granted to specific individuals or it may be granted to a group of individuals, such as all PIV cardholders, or all PIV cardholders sponsored by a specific agency. If authorization is granted to specific individuals, information about the cardholder (see Section 6.1) must be added to the PACS server's authorization database. However, when authorization is granted to a group of individuals, adding information about individual cardholders may not be necessary, as the PACS may be able to determine on-the-fly whether a cardholder belongs to an authorized group (see Appendix D). For example, if every PIV cardholder sponsored by Agency X is authorized to enter through the main entrance to Agency

---

deprecated and continues to be mandatory. In addition to being the only data element in which the optional Cardholder UUID appears, [FIPS201] permits the CHUID data element to be used in the BIO(-A) and SYM-CAK authentication mechanisms as a source for the card's expiration date and for a unique identifier from the PIV Card.

[18] Unlike non-Federal issuers of PIV-I cards, Federal agencies that are assigned agency codes in [SP800-87] may use their agency codes to assign FASC-Ns for PIV-I cards in a manner that ensures their uniqueness.

X's headquarters, then the PACS may grant access if the presented PIV Card can be authenticated and the Agency Code in the card's FASC-N is the code for Agency X.

PACS registration occurs when information about the cardholder is stored by the PACS for later use when the individual's PIV Card is presented at an access point. The information that a PACS stores aids in authenticating the cardholder. Many PACS require that cardholders be preregistered, i.e., be registered with the PACS before their PIV Cards are submitted at access points. While these guidelines do not require preregistration, preregistration is strongly recommended since it can make the authentication process faster and more reliable.

In most cases, information about the PIV Card will be collected at the same time that the cardholder's identifier is added to the PACS' authorization database, but collection of card information may be performed separately. For example, an agency may have an access point for which all Federal employees are authorized access. The agency may automatically register information about the PIV Cards that it issues in the PACS, and then set up self-registration kiosks for employees of other agencies. Before trying to enter the access point for the first time, non-agency cardholders would present their PIV Cards at one of the kiosks, which would validate the card, verify that the cardholder is a Federal employee, and then collect whatever information the PACS needs to facilitate authenticating the cardholder when the cardholder presents the card at the access point.

While the PACS might not need to store any information about the cardholder, if online credential validation is performed by the PACS at the time of each authentication (see Section 4.4), credential validation can be time consuming. If a PIV Card is preregistered, then the credentials on the card can be validated when the card is registered, so that they don't need to be validated when the card is presented at an access point. A caching status proxy (see Section 4.4) may be employed to locally store the status of cardholders' authentication certificates and provide that information to relying parties when needed. Where one-factor authentication is sufficient, the Card Authentication may be used. Where at least two-factor authentication is required, the PIV Authentication certificate should be used.

When the individual is registered using a caching status proxy, the registration station obtains the PIV Authentication or Card Authentication certificate from the PIV Card, validates the certificate (including checking the certificate's revocation status), and sends a challenge to the card to verify that it holds the private key corresponding to the certificate. The authentication certificate is then added to the server's database, along with any other information about the individual that the server maintains (e.g., the individual's authorizations). This process is used for one or both credentials, depending on the PIV Authentication mechanism supported by the PACS.

Since certificate revocation is used as a mechanism to indicate that a PIV Card should no longer be considered valid, the caching status proxy should periodically revalidate all of the certificates in its database and deactivate the access privileges of any individual whose certificate has expired or has been revoked. Revalidation should be performed by the caching status proxy at least once per day. Once the decision has been made to revoke a PIV Card, agencies may employ local deauthorization methods to supplement certificate revocation and achieve a more rapid local effect.

Recommendation 6.1: The CHUID data object may be collected at registration, but it should not be retained. Data elements (e.g., the FASC-N and Global Unique Identifier (GUID)) may be extracted from the CHUID and retained, as may a hash of the CHUID. NIST strongly recommends against the storage of complete CHUIDs in relying systems.

Recommendation 6.2: PKI-AUTH and PKI-CAK authentication mechanisms should be implemented by a PACS reader[19] capable of full certificate path validation, either online or using a caching status proxy. Agencies should consider using online status checks when the most up to date PIV Card status is necessary or if access is being granted to Exclusion areas. If a caching status proxy is used, the certificates should be captured when the PIV Card is registered with the PACS.

6.3   Role-Based Access Control

Authorization of identities enrolled in a PACS is viewed as separate from cardholder authentication. PACS may grant access only to cardholders who were registered and authorized in the PACS server prior to presenting their credentials for authentication, or they may make on-the-fly[20] access control decisions by evaluating the information on presented PIV Cards against a set of access control rules. Because PIV Cards contain only a few mandatory subject attributes (just the Agency Code, Employee Affiliation, and Investigation Status Indicator) that may be used for role-based access control, role or group permissions will usually be derived from off-card information.

Recommendation 6.3: Because having on-card role and permission information would raise difficult challenges concerning update and revocation, PACS permissions should generally be stored in a PACS facilities-based component, such as a panel or controller database.

6.4   Disaster Response and Recovery Incidents

In addition to the use of a PIV credential for cardholder authentication during routine everyday use, the PIV credentials may also be used for access to federal facilities and federally controlled areas internal to disaster response and recovery incident scenes. Federal agencies should consider access for personnel from agencies with responsibilities under the National Response Framework, National Incident Management System, National Infrastructure Protection Plan, and the National Continuity Policy Implementation Plan when identifying and categorizing PACS perimeters as protecting Controlled, Limited, and Exclusion areas. Subsequently, agencies should apply appropriate (in accordance with Table 4-3) PIV authentication mechanisms to the areas to ensure that incident management personnel, emergency response providers, and other personnel (including temporary personnel) and resources likely needed to respond to a natural

---

[19] Note that in this document, a PACS reader's authentication capabilities is assumed to be support by a PACS controller since the controller is usually the component to execute or support execution of the PIV authentication mechanisms, while the reader functions as the interface between the PIV Card and the controller.

[20] Although making on-the-fly access control decisions is acceptable, it should be noted that this could introduce considerable delay in the end-user authorization process; and is therefore not recommended.

disaster, act of terrorism, or other manmade disaster can be electronically authenticated in order to attain movement internal to federally controlled facilities and areas within the incident scene.

6.5   Temporary Badges

[HSPD-12] mandated a common identification and verification standard for federal employees and contractors for physical access to federally controlled facilities and logical access to federally controlled information systems. OMB Memorandum M-05-24 [M-05-24] and the Final Credentialing Standards for Issuance Personal Identity Verification Cards under HSPD-12 [OPM Memo] issued by the Office of Personnel Management (OPM) clarifies the eligibility requirements for a PIV Card. Temporary employees and contractors are those individuals employed for 6 months or less. These individuals are not required to receive a PIV Card and agencies are permitted to issue non-PIV Cards to these individuals. In addition, PIV cardholders who have forgotten their cards may be issued a non-PIV Card on a temporary basis. Temporary badges will thus be necessary (in smaller numbers than before) for the indefinite future.

An agency or facility should consider the relationship of temporary badges to PIV Cards and their PACS system(s) when selecting temporary badge products. Factors to consider during the procurement process include:

+   The [M-05-24] requirement that temporary badges be visually and electronically distinguishable from PIV Cards.

+   Capabilities and costs of enrollment stations, which will likely be local to the facility for best turnaround time.

+   The interoperability of temporary badges with PIV readers and authentication mechanisms (especially PKI-CAK for physical access).

+   The assignment of unique identifiers (FASC-N or UUID) to temporary badges, to foster interoperability with PIV readers.

+   The suitability of contactless-only temporary badges for physical access.

+   The performance, cost, and security tradeoffs between disposable and reusable temporary badges.

Many approaches to temporary badges are possible. However, a smart-card based solution that leverages current infrastructure and interoperates with federal PIV Card readers and their applications is recommended.

6.6   Lost PIV Card or Suspicion of Fraudulent Use

If a lost PIV Card is found by a person other than the cardholder, or if a pattern of PIV Card activity raises suspicions of fraudulent use, the security office of the issuing agency, or of the cardholder's duty station, should be notified. The security office (issuing and local duty station) will determine if further investigation is warranted and if the PCI should be asked to revoke the PIV Card.

6.7   PACS and ICAM Infrastructure

A PACS should be integrated with the agency's overall ICAM infrastructure, such as with the enterprise identity management and credentialing systems to provision authoritative identity and credential information and to shared PKI validation components. An integrated PACS enables information sharing across systems and agencies with common access controls and policies. The agency's ICAM infrastructure would serve as the central Chain of Trust of identity that many applications can trust and consume authorization decisions—specifically applications that leverage PIV for physical and logical access.

Appendix A — An Overview of PIV Authentication Mechanisms

PIV authentication mechanisms offer a range of security measures that can be applied in a PACS environment. This Appendix describes each of the PIV Authentication mechanism in further details.

A.1   Authentication using PIV Visual Credentials (VIS)

Visual authentication entails inspection of the topographical features on the front and back of the PIV Card. The human guard checks to see that the PIV Card looks genuine, compares the cardholder's facial features with the picture on the card, checks the expiration date printed on the card, verifies the correctness of other data elements printed on the card, and visually verifies the security feature(s) on the card. The effectiveness of this mechanism depends on the training, skill, and diligence of the guard (to match the face in spite of changes in physical appearance – beard, mustache, hair coloring, eye glasses, etc.) – counterfeit IDs can pass visual inspections easily. Digital scanners, printers, and image editing software have made counterfeiting easier. Moreover, the visual verification of security features does not scale well across agencies since each agency may implement different security features. For these reasons, [FIPS201] has downgraded this authentication mechanism to indicate that it provides "LITTLE or NO" confidence in the identity of the cardholder.

A.2   Authentication using the Cardholder Unique Identifier (CHUID)

The CHUID, as defined in [FIPS201] and [TIG SEPACS], is one of the mandatory data objects on PIV Cards. The CHUID contains two data elements, the FASC-N and the Card UUID, that uniquely identify the PIV Card. The CHUID also uniquely identifies an individual since each PIV Card is issued to an individual. The CHUID data object is signed by the issuer so alterations or modifications to a CHUID can be detected. An expired CHUID, failure of signature verification or path validation results in a failed authentication attempt that does not admit a cardholder for access.

The CHUID is a free read object on the PIV Card; and thus, it can be read or cloned easily. Because of the risk of cloning, the CHUID authentication mechanism provides "LITTLE or NO" confidence in the identity of the cardholder. For this reason, the CHUID authentication mechanism has been deprecated in [FIPS201] and is expected to be removed in a future revision of the standard.

A.3   Authentication with the Card Authentication Certificate (PKI-CAK)

The asymmetric Card Authentication key, as defined in [FIPS201], is one of two mandatory asymmetric authentication keys present on the PIV Card. As the name implies, the purpose of the PKI-CAK authentication mechanism is to authenticate the card and therefore its possessor. Unlike the CHUID authentication mechanism, the PKI-CAK authentication mechanism is highly resistant to cloning, since cloning would require obtaining a copy of the private key. PKI-CAK also provides protection against use of a revoked card as authentication fails and cardholder access is denied when certificate validation indicates that the certificate has been revoked. Similarly, failed signature verification or path validation results in a failed authentication attempt that does not admit a cardholder for access.

The PKI-CAK authentication mechanism is unique among the PIV authentication mechanisms since it is the only PIV authentication mechanism that provides at least SOME confidence in the identity of the cardholder that can be performed over the contactless interface using only card features that are mandatory under [FIPS201].

> **Recommendation A.1:** NIST recommends using the PKI-CAK authentication mechanism at access points that only require single-factor authentication.

A.4 Authentication with the Symmetric Card Authentication Key (SYM-CAK)

The SYM-CAK authentication mechanism is similar to the PKI-CAK authentication mechanism, except that it uses the optional symmetric Card Authentication key to authenticate the card and it does not provide protection against use of a revoked card. Due to its optionality and its use of a single symmetric key that needs to be shared, stored and protected with reader components, SYM-CAK is not suited for interoperable authentication mechanism as mandated by [HSPD-12], and therefore is only suitable for use in authenticating PIV Cards issued by the same agency that operates the PACS.

A.5 Unattended Authentication Using Off-Card Biometric Comparison (BIO)

PACS may perform off-card biometric authentication using the fingerprint information or the optional iris images stored on the PIV Card.[21] The biometric on the PIV Card is signed by the issuer, so the authenticity of the biometric can be checked by the PACS. Verification of the signature on the biometric data object and matching of the reference biometric template with the sample biometric template, is performed by the PACS application. The verification of signature and matching of biometric results in one-factor authentication. This authentication mechanism does not include authentication of the PIV Card.

Potentially, a biometric template could be placed on a fake card – so neither the "something you have" nor "something you know" factors are validated. As a result, this document rates the BIO authentication mechanism as a one-factor ("something you are") authentication mechanism. BIO combined with a cryptographic challenge/response authenticates the PIV Card and thus achieves three-factor authentication (see Section A.9).

> **Recommendation A.2:** Biometric readers, especially those used at access points to Limited and Exclusion areas, should have a proven capability to accept live fingers and reject artificial fingers. Biometric readers, especially unattended readers in an Unrestricted area, should be physically hardened to protect against direct electrical compromise.

A.6 Attended Authentication Using Off-Card Biometric Comparison (BIO-A)

The BIO-A authentication mechanism is the same as BIO authentication but an attendant supervises the use of the PIV Card and the submission of the PIN and the sample biometric by

---

[21] As noted in Section 4.2.3.1 of [FIPS201], neither the fingerprint templates nor the iris images are guaranteed to be present on a PIV Card, since it may not be possible to collect fingerprints from some cardholders and iris images collection is optional. When biometric authentication cannot be performed, PKI-AUTH is the recommended alternate authentication mechanism. Agency security policy may require additional authentication mechanisms in consideration of impact-based security management.

the cardholder. Some fingerprint biometric readers have been shown to accept fake or synthetic fingerprints; others may allow access to internal wiring with relative ease. The presence of an attendant during BIO-A authentication serves to mitigate these risks. Moreover, the presence of an attendant also provides increased assurance, relative to BIO, that a fake card is not being used, which accounts for an additional authentication factor of "something you have." Since the PIN is verified by the PIV Card and the card itself is not verified by PACS, the "something you know" authentication factor is not validated. In summary, the BIO-A authentication mechanism benefits from a presence of an attendant, but not from a strong challenge/response authentication, with the PIV Card. Therefore, BIO-A is considered a two-factor authentication mechanism.

A.7   Authentication with the PIV Authentication Certificate (PKI-AUTH)

The PIV Authentication key, as defined in [FIPS201], is a mandatory asymmetric key present on the PIV Card. A PACS that performs public key cryptography-based authentication with the PIV Authentication key uses the PKI-AUTH authentication mechanism. Use of PKI-AUTH provides two-factor authentication, since the cardholder must present the card (something you have) and either enter a PIN (something you know) or submit a fingerprint (something you are) to unlock the card in order to successfully authenticate.

Similar to the PKI-CAK authentication mechanism, the PKI-AUTH authentication mechanism involves validation of the PIV Authentication certificate. The validation protects against use of a revoked card as authentication fails and cardholder access is denied when certificate validation indicates that the certificate has been revoked. Similarly, failed signature verification or path validation results in a failed authentication attempt that does not admit a cardholder for access.

A.8   Authentication Using On-Card Biometric Comparison (OCC-AUTH)

The PIV Card may optionally implement on-card biometric comparison (OCC). With OCC, biometric comparison data is stored on the card and cannot be read but may be used by the card to authenticate the cardholder.

The OCC-AUTH authentication mechanism is implemented by performing OCC over secure messaging. The PACS authenticates the PIV Card as part of the process of establishing secure messaging, and the response from the PIV Card indicating that OCC was successful can be verified since the response includes a message authentication code. Therefore, OCC-AUTH provides two-factor authentication – something you have (i.e., the card via establishment of the secure messaging protocol with the PACS application) and something you are (i.e., a fingerprint via OCC). The OCC-AUTH authentication mechanism is highly resistant to cloning. However, it does not protect against use of a revoked card. Additionally, not all PIV Cards support OCC-AUTH, as both secure messaging and OCC are optionally card capabilities. The recommendations in Section A.5 also apply to OCC-AUTH.

A.9   (PKI-CAK | SYM-CAK) + BIO(-A) Authentication

Three-factor authentication may be achieved by combining BIO(-A) with either PKI-CAK or SYM-CAK. In this case, the PKI-CAK or SYM-CAK authentication mechanism is used to authenticate the PIV Card and therefore the entry of the PIN to access the biometric fingerprint template can now be trusted.

As with the PKI-CAK authentication mechanism when performed alone, the PKI-CAK + BIO(-A) authentication mechanism is highly resistant to cloning. The mechanism also protects against the use of a revoked card as the authentication fails, and the cardholder is denied access when certificate validation indicates that the PIV Card has been revoked. SYM-CAK + BIO(-A) is also highly resistant to cloning but does not protect against the use of a revoked card. Unlike PKI-CAK, SYM-CAK relies on an optional PIV Card feature, so the SYM-CAK + BIO(-A) authentication mechanism does not support interagency interoperability.

Appendix B —Combinations of PIV Authentication Mechanisms in PACS

Section 4.3 provides recommendations for selecting the authentication mechanisms to use at access points. For access to Controlled areas, it considers any PIV authentication mechanism that provides at least SOME confidence in the identity of the cardholder to be acceptable (see Table 6-2 in [FIPS201]). For access to Limited areas, it recommends use of a PIV authentication mechanism that provides either HIGH or VERY HIGH confidence in the identity of the cardholder (see Table 6-2 in [FIPS201]). It also recommends that the single-factor BIO authentication mechanism only be used to grant access to a Limited area if the PACS can ensure that the cardholder needed to authenticate at another access point with a different authentication mechanism in order to get to the Limited access point (authentication in context). For access to Exclusion areas, it recommends use of a PIV authentication mechanism that provides for at least two-factor authentication at the access point (see Table 4-1), and that the PACS ensure that all three factors are authenticated prior to granting access to Exclusion area (possibly through authentication in context).

This appendix provides a complete list of possible PIV authentication mechanism combinations that are available for application to federal facilities. The following acronyms are used in this appendix, where each acronym represents the set of PIV authentication mechanisms that provide the specified factor(s) of authentication.

Acronym	PIV Authentication Mechanisms
H (One factor – something you have)	PKI-CAK, SYM-CAK
A (One factor – something you are)	BIO
HK (Two factors – something you have, something you know)	PKI-AUTH (with PIN)
HA (Two factors – something you have, something you are)	BIO-A, OCC-AUTH, PKI-AUTH (with OCC)
HKA (Three factors – something you have, something you know, something you are)	PKI-CAK+BIO(-A), SYM-CAK+BIO(-A))

Note that the table above only lists individual PIV authentication mechanisms that correspond to each acronym, except for the combinations as identified in Section 4.2. However, other PIV authentication mechanism combinations that provide the same set of authentication factors can be derived. For combined authentication mechanisms, it is assumed that the combination is completed using the same interface. For example, in the case of SYM-CAK+BIO, both SYM-CAK and BIO would need to be performed over the contact interface, since BIO is performed over the contact interface as per Table 4-1.

When an access point separates a protective area from an Unrestricted area or when authentication in context cannot be used, Section 4.3 recommends that one of the following be used:

- For access to a Controlled area – any authentication mechanism listed above (H, A, HK, HA, or HKA)

- For access to a Limited area – any two- or three-factor authentication mechanism listed above (HK, HA, or HKA)

- For access to an Exclusion area – any three-factor authentication mechanism listed above (HKA)

The tables below show all possible PIV authentication mechanism combinations that may be used when authentication in context can be utilized. The first table shows all possible options for accessing a Limited area when the Limited area can only be accessed from within a Controlled area. It shows that if only "something you are" was authenticated to access the Controlled area (row 2), then the options for granting access to the Limited area are the same as if authentication in context were not available, however, if "something you have" is authenticated to access the Controlled area (row 1), then there is the additional option of only authenticating "something you are" (BIO) before granting access to the Limited area.

	Access Point A (Controlled)	Access Point B (Limited)
1	H, HK, HA, or HKA	A, HK, HA, or HKA
2	A	HK, HA, or HKA

The second table shows all possible combinations when a facility has Controlled, Limited, and Exclusion areas, Limited areas can only be accessed from within Controlled areas, and Exclusion areas can only be accessed from within Limited areas.

	Access Point A (Controlled)	Access Point B (Limited)	Access Point C (Exclusion)
1	H	A or HA	HK or HKA
2	H	HK	HA or HKA
3	H	HKA	HK, HA, or HKA
4	A	HK or HKA	HK, HA, or HKA
5	A	HA	HK or HKA
6	HK	A, HA, or HKA	HK, HA, or HKA
7	HK	HK	HA or HKA
8	HA	A or HA	HK or HKA
9	HA	HK or HKA	HK, HA, or HKA
10	HKA	A, HK, HA, or HKA	HK, HA, or HKA

The "Access Point C" column shows the authentication mechanisms that can be used to access an Exclusion area given the authentication mechanisms used to access the surrounding Controlled and Limited areas (the "Access Point A" and "Access Point B" columns). For example, rows 4 and 5 show (as did row 2 in the first table) that if only "something you are" was authenticated to access the Controlled area, then two- or three-factor authentication is required at the Limited access point (HK, HA, or HKA). Row 4 shows that if HK or HKA is used at the Limited access point after A (i.e., BIO) is used at the Controlled access point, then any two- or three-factor authentication mechanism may be used at an Exclusion access point, whereas row 5 shows that if HA is used at the Limited access point after A (i.e., BIO) is used at the Controlled access point, then "something you know" needs to be authenticated at the Exclusion access point (HK or HKA).

The third and fourth tables show all combinations in cases in which authentication in context can be used, but there are access points that separate areas that differ by more than one impact level. The third table shows the combinations for cases in which Exclusion areas can be accessed from within Controlled areas, and the fourth table shows combinations for cases in which Limited areas can be accessed from Unrestricted areas and Exclusion areas can be accessed from within those Limited areas.

	Access Point A (Controlled)	Access Point B (Exclusion)
1	H	HKA
2	A or HA	HK or HKA
3	HK	HA or HKA
4	HKA	HK, HA, or HKA

	Access Point A (Limited)	Access Point B (Exclusion)
1	HK	HA or HKA
2	HA	HK or HKA
3	HKA	HK, HA, or HKA

Appendix C — Improving Authentication Transaction Times

The deprecation of the CHUID authentication mechanism marks the end for authentication based on reading a static identifier. With the deprecation, however, PACS systems lose a mechanism that is by nature fast. The PKI-CAK authentication mechanism is the most logical replacement for the CHUID authentication mechanism, is computationally expensive. To approach transaction times closer to the CHUID authentication mechanism, optimizations are needed within the PIV Cards as well as with the readers and associated infrastructure. Transaction times for other authentication mechanisms are also important, and many of the recommendations in this section apply to other PIV authentication mechanisms as well.

The steps of the PKI-CAK authentication mechanism can be described as follows:

- The reader obtains information from the PIV Card that allows it to determine an identifier for the card and to determine the card's Card Authentication certificate.

- The reader sends a challenge string to the PIV Card and requests an asymmetric operation in response.

- The card responds to the previously issued challenge by signing it using the Card Authentication private key.

- The relying system (reader or controller) uses the public key from the Card Authentication certificate to verify the response from the card.

- The relying system verifies that the Card Authentication certificate is valid.

- The relying system uses the identifier from the card to make an access control decision.

Each of the steps above presents an opportunity for optimization.

As a starting point, PCIs should consider performance when purchasing card stock, as the card is involved in four of the six steps above. When the PKI-CAK authentication mechanism is performed, the PIV Card needs to perform a power-on self-test, perform a private key signature operation using the Card Authentication private key, and transmit data to the reader, so the performance of all of these steps is relevant to the overall performance of the card. [SP800-78] allows the Card Authentication key to be either a 2048-bit RSA key or an elliptic curve cryptography (ECC) P-256 key, and many cards support both cryptographic algorithms. When a card supports both algorithms, the performance of both algorithms should be considered.

> **Recommendation C.1**: Since ECC private key operations are generally faster than RSA private key operations, PCIs should consider issuing PIV Cards with ECC Card Authentication keys rather than RSA.

The performance of the PIV Card is partially dependent upon the reader. The PKI-CAK authentication mechanism is usually performed over the contactless interface, with the PIV Card being powered by the reader's magnetic field, and cards will operate more slowly when they are underpowered. Improper installation of the reader may lead to the card being underpowered, and it may also create interference that makes communication between the card and the reader unreliable, which would also lead to increased transaction times.

> **Recommendation C.2**: Make use of Qualified HSPD-12 Service Providers[22] to ensure that PACS components are properly installed and that readers are properly tested and tuned to provide optimal performance.

In order to maximize performance, the PIV Card needs to be held correctly within the reader's magnetic field. So, departments and agencies should provide information to their cardholders on the proper way to present their cards to the readers. Placing an image on the reader depicting the proper orientation of the card may also be helpful.

Preregistration of PIV Cards can help to speed up many of the steps in the PKI-CAK authentication mechanism. If the card's Card Authentication certificate was obtained during the preregistration process then it doesn't need to be read from the card at the time of authentication.[23] Instead, the reader can obtain an identifier from the card (e.g., by reading the initial portion of the CHUID and extracting the FASC-N, Card UUD, or Cardholder UUID) and can then use the identifier to look up the certificate in the local cache. In addition, status information for the Card Authentication certificate may be obtained from a caching status proxy rather than performing certificate validation at the time of authentication.[24]

In many PACS systems, data is transferred from the reader to the controller using the Wiegand protocol, which is very slow and only allows for one-way communication. Replacing the cabling between the reader and the controller to support fast two-way communication will provide several benefits: it will speed up the transfer of the card's identifier from the reader to the controller; it will enable the caching of the Card Authentication certificate at the controller; and it will allow the reader to offload more of the processing to the controller. Given that card readers tend to have very little processing power, it may be more efficient, if fast two-way communication is available, for the reader to send the results of the challenge to the controller rather than performing the signature verification itself.

> **Recommendation C.3**: Consider the benefits of upgrading the communications infrastructure between readers and controllers and then using the improved communication to move processing steps to the component that can perform the step most efficiently.

---

[22] Information about Qualified HSPD-12 Service Providers can be found at https://www.idmanagement.gov/IDM/s/article_detail?link=list-of-certified-services.

[23] The PACS should be prepared to handle cases in which the Card Authentication certificate on the card was replaced (due to re-key) after the card was preregistered.

[24] Agencies should consider using online status checks when the most up to date PIV Card status is necessary.

Appendix D — FASC-N Uniqueness

Once the user has been authenticated, access control decisions can be made by comparing PIV identifiers (see Section 6.1) against the ACL entries. While any of the PIV identifiers may be used in making access control decisions, within the limitations described in Section 6.1, this appendix discusses the use of the FASC-N, or portions of the FASC-N, for making access control decisions.

Three components of the FASC-N, the Agency Code, System Code, and Credential Number, constitute the FASC-N Identifier. An individual's FASC-N Identifier is unique among all cardholders when the complete three-element subset of the FASC-N is used for comparison. There will be no collisions since all of the cardholders have been assigned unique numbers. An ACL pattern may match the entire FASC-N, just the Agency Code, or the Agency Code and System Code (e.g., all PIV Cards issued to one agency, or to one site in one agency) without introducing dangerous collisions or ambiguities across agencies. The values of additional FASC-N fields may be included in the identifiers that are compared against the ACL entries.

This restricts the access control comparison to one of three cases when using the FASC-N:

1. the Agency Code alone (i.e., all PIV Cards with the same Agency Code are accepted);

2. the Agency Code and System Code only (i.e., all PIV Card with the same Agency Code and System Code are accepted); or

3. the Agency Code, System Code, and Credential Number (i.e., a uniquely identified PIV Card).

Any of these cases may also include comparison of additional FASC-N values such as the Credential Series, Individual Credential Issue, Organizational Identifier, or Person Identifier.[25]

The FASC-N data fields are defined as fixed length values of Binary Coded Decimal digits. The complete subset of three data fields is 14 decimal digits in length, as stored on the PIV Card. Other representations of the FASC-N Identifier, for example a binary representation, may be used off card, provided that they are isomorphic with respect to pattern matching. The following examples demonstrate the possible uses of FASC-N in a PIV-enabled PACS application.

D.1   Full FASC-N Comparison

The following table shows a successful match against an ACL pattern consisting of a full FASC-N comparison. These examples show an organization-specific access control policy that includes the comparison of all FASC-N fields.

---

[25] [SP800-73] allows issuers to populate the FASC-N's Credential Series, Individual Credential Issue, Organizational Identifier, and Person Identifier fields with all zeros, so these fields may not always provide useful information for comparison.

FIELD NAME	PIV Card FASC-N	ACL FASC-N Pattern
Agency Code	3728	3728
System Code	8377	8377
Credential Number	123456	123456
Credential Series	1	1
Individual Credential Issue	1	1
Person Identifier	1234567890	1234567890
Organizational Category	1	1
Organizational Identifier	0010	0010
Person/Organization Association Category	1	1

The following table shows an unsuccessful match against an ACL pattern consisting of full FASC-N comparison.

FIELD NAME	PIV Card FASC-N	ACL FASC-N Pattern
Agency Code	3728	3728
System Code	8377	8377
Credential Number	123456	234567
Credential Series	1	1
Individual Credential Issue	1	1
Person Identifier	1234567890	1234567890
Organizational Category	1	1
Organizational Identifier	0010	0010
Person/Organization Association Category	1	1

D.2   FASC-N Identifier Comparison

The following table shows a successful match against an ACL pattern consisting of one specific
FASC-N Identifier.

FIELD NAME	PIV Card FASC-N	ACL FASC-N Pattern
Agency Code	3728	3728
System Code	8377	8377
Credential Number	123456	123456

The following table shows an unsuccessful match against an ACL pattern consisting of one
specific FASC-N Identifier.

FIELD NAME	PIV Card FASC-N	ACL FASC-N Pattern
Agency Code	3728	3728
System Code	8367	8377
Credential Number	123456	123456

D.3   Partial FASC-N Comparison

The following table shows a successful match against an ACL pattern consisting of an Agency
Code and the System Code. The "x" symbols represent "don't care" decimal digits.

FIELD NAME	PIV Card FASC-N	ACL FASC-N Pattern
Agency Code	3728	3728
System Code	8391	8391
Credential Number	654321	xxxxxx

The following table shows an unsuccessful match against an ACL pattern consisting of an
Agency Code and the System Code.

FIELD NAME	PIV Card FASC-N	ACL FASC-N Pattern
Agency Code	3628	3728
System Code	8377	8377

Credential Number	123456	xxxxxx

The following table shows a disallowed pattern that is not an initial string of the FASC-N Identifier.

FIELD NAME	PIV Card FASC-N	ACL FASC-N Pattern
Agency Code	3728	37xx
System Code	8377	83xx
Credential Number	123456	xxxxxx

D.4   Isomorphic FASC-N Comparison

The following table shows a successful match against an ACL pattern, with the FASC-N Identifier and the upper and lower bounds of the ACL pattern represented in hexadecimal. The match succeeds because the presented FASC-N Identifier is in the closed interval [LB, UB]. This example is the same as the MATCH example of D.2, with a shift in representation from decimal to hexadecimal.

FIELD VALUE	PIV Card FASC-N	ACL Pattern LB	ACL Pattern UB
Hexadecimal Value	21E9E156BBB1	21E9DBE03300	21E9E1D613FF

The following table shows an unsuccessful match against an ACL pattern, with the FASC-N Identifier and the upper and lower bounds of the ACL pattern represented in hexadecimal. The match fails because the presented FASC-N Identifier is not in the closed interval [LB, UB]. This example is the same as the NO MATCH example of D.2, with a shift in representation from decimal to hexadecimal.

FIELD VALUE	PIV Card FASC-N	ACL Pattern LB	ACL Pattern UB
Hexadecimal Value	21010BD3F280	21E9DBE03300	21E9E1D613FF

Appendix E — Limitations of Legacy Physical Access Control Systems

[FIPS201] and its supporting special publications impose specific requirements on PACS interfaces with PIV Card and PIV System. These requirements presented technical challenges in migrating to PIV Card use in the areas of cardholder identification, card-to-reader interface, and authentication protocol. The following sections explore how [FIPS201] requirements differ from the capabilities of PACS that are not PIV-enabled.

E.1   Cardholder Identification

Legacy PACS use cards with data formats that are often proprietary to the specific enterprise. Many of the legacy PACS use an ID number based on a 26-bit standard, which is comprised of an 8-bit site code and a 16-bit unique card ID number with 2 bits assigned to parity (the parity bits add confidence that the data transmission has no errors). The 8-bit site code accommodates 256 unique sites and the 16-bit card ID number accommodates 65 536 unique users for that site. Larger ID numbers are used by some legacy systems but they are not necessarily interoperable.

A PACS based on the 26-bit format is deployed as a standalone solution at a dedicated site. Typically, these solutions are managed locally, and an individual with an access card for one site cannot use the same card at a second site and must obtain a second card. [FIPS201] changes this dynamic because the credential is issued through a separate process instead of as part of the PACS deployment. Legacy PACS need to be upgraded or re-provisioned to support at least a 14-decimal-digit FASC-N Identifier or a 16-byte Card UUID (see Appendix D).

E.2   Door Reader Interface

PACS readers come in varying configurations and offer multiple interface options for the card and the controller. [FIPS201] standardizes the use of the [ISO/IEC 14443] interface for the contactless reader to card communication. Note that the card reader may require additional conformance testing for federal acquisition. An authority for such conformance testing is the General Services Administration (GSA) FIPS 201 Evaluation Program [FIPS 201 EP], which defines tests and maintains a list of approved products. Not all existing PACS use this interface, so some agencies may have to plan to migrate from their legacy environment to the [ISO/IEC 14443] conformant interface. Alternatively, an agency may use the PIV Card's contact interface based on [ISO/IEC 7816].

The interface from the door reader to the controller also comes in different configurations. [FIPS201] does not specify which protocols can be used for this interface, as long as the necessary data can be communicated to the controller. Typical deployed implementations support transmitting a small amount of data (on the order of 10 to 15 bytes), but [FIPS201] defines data elements that are much larger. Therefore, depending on the agency's implementation strategy, an upgrade to the door reader to controller interface may also be required. At a minimum, a 14-decimal-digit FASC-N Identifier or the full 16-byte Card UUID will be supported. Note that any change to this interface may also necessitate changes to the physical wiring and cabling infrastructures.

E.3   Authentication Capability

Legacy PACS readers use proximity or magnetic stripe technology to interface with identity cards and use proprietary protocols to communicate data. Some of these proprietary protocols employ cryptography, but their use is limited to the local site. [FIPS201] specifies identity credentials that can be used for a new generation of identity management technology for building access. [FIPS201] and its supporting special publications define the credential data model and the card-to-reader interface, and also provide requirements for implementing the digital certificates.

[FIPS201] added a standardized contactless and contact interface, PIN, biometric fingerprints, optional iris images, and cryptography to the card that could be used to attain a higher level of identity authentication assurance. The capability to perform bi-directional data communication is fundamental to the deployment of secure building access. Adding cryptography to the cards permits agencies to validate the data objects on the card and authenticate the cardholder. Adding credential expiration and credential validation requirements also strengthens access control decisions. At the same time, [FIPS201] provided the opportunity to migrate building access systems from LITTLE or NO confidence levels to VERY HIGH confidence levels. Legacy PACS may need upgrades to take advantage of these features and functions, in coordination with the following guidelines and authorities:

+   [FIPS201] assurance levels.

+   The Risk Management Process for Federal Facilities: An Interagency Security Committee Standard [ISC-RMP].

[FIPS201] redefines the requirements for building access in a fundamental way: instead of each facility issuing an access card solely for that facility's PACS architecture, a facility relies on the PIV Card that was issued by the same, or a different, agency certified by the Federal Government. The facility still has control over the user's access privileges, but the technology has been standardized to optimize interagency interoperability and the credential has been issued to the user as part of the [FIPS201] identity management process.

E.4   Wiring

Selecting a particular reader type and its interface with the controller requires careful attention to wiring. Existing wiring should be assessed for its ability to meet the requirements of new readers and controllers, taking performance into consideration. The existing wiring may be a limiting factor due to its capacity to transmit data and original specifications. Many recently installed systems use higher bandwidth cables, which are typically sufficient for a PIV-based access control system. In some environments, advanced signaling methods operating at higher speeds with lower signal-to-noise margins can necessitate upgrades to the wiring.

E.5   Software Upgrades

Vendors may be able to upgrade their PACS software to minimize the hardware changes needed for a legacy PACS to accept PIV Cards. Software or firmware upgrades to controllers or door readers may be available to agencies. PACS suppliers should be asked if software or firmware upgrades supporting PIV Cards are a possibility. If available, the agency should ensure that the software upgrade will have no adverse effect on the PACS system or any interconnected systems.

E.6 Legacy PACS Cards and PIV Card Differences

The list below compares the basic differences in the technology offerings between the legacy PACS cards and the PIV Card.

+ Some legacy PACS use site-specific card technology, with the result that a card cannot be used at sites with incompatible PACS. For example, a magnetic stripe card cannot be used at a proximity card site, and a magnetic stripe card from one vendor cannot be used at a site with magnetic stripe equipment from another vendor.

+ Legacy PACS cards can provide an identifying number, but in most cases, they cannot respond to a cryptographic challenge. Many non-PIV PACS cards can be copied easily.

+ When two sites use compatible legacy card technology, the risk of duplicate site identifiers for cards is always present. Without government-wide coordination of identifiers, the same identifier could be used on multiple cards at different sites.

+ To achieve government-wide coordination of cardholder identifiers, enough identifiers must be available for all government-issued credentials. Many legacy PACS have a limit on the number of sites (256) and the number of users per site (65 536) that is too small for government-wide use and can lead to the same identifiers being issued to different individuals.

+ Legacy PACS control expiration of credentials through an expiration date stored in a site database, whereas with PIV Cards, expiration dates can be obtained from the cards themselves. There is no simple way to synchronize the expiration of credentials for a federal employee or contractor with access to multiple sites unless all sites are tied into a centralized enterprise-wide PACS (e-PACS).

+ Use of PINs, public key infrastructure, and biometrics with legacy PACS is managed on a site-specific basis at the PACS server. Individuals must enroll PINs, keys, or biometrics at each site. Since PINs, keys, and biometrics are often stored in a site database, they may not be technically interoperable with the requirements of other sites.

[FIPS201]-conformant PIV-enabled PACS eliminate or substantially reduce each of these limitations, relative to legacy PACS installations.

Appendix F — References

[FIPS199]   Federal Information Processing Standard 199, *Standards for Security Categorization of Federal Information and Information System*, February 2004. https://doi.org/10.6028/NIST.FIPS.199.

[FIPS201]   Federal Information Processing Standard 201-2, *Personal Identity Verification (PIV) of Federal Employees and Contractors*, August 2013. https://doi.org/10.6028/NIST.FIPS.201-2.

[FIPS 201 EP] *FIPS 201 Evaluation Program.* https://www.idmanagement.gov/fips201/ [accessed 5/16/18].

[FISMA]   *Federal Information Security Modernization Act of 2014*, Pub. L. 113-283, 128 Stat 3073. https://www.congress.gov/113/plaws/publ283/PLAW-113publ283.pdf [accessed 5/16/18].

[HSPD-12]   Homeland Security Presidential Directive 12, *Policy for a Common Identification Standard for Federal Employees and Contractors*, August 27, 2004. https://www.dhs.gov/homeland-security-presidential-directive-12 [accessed 5/16/18]

[ISC-RMP]   *The Risk Management Process for Federal Facilities: An Interagency Security Committee Standard*, 2nd edition, November 2016. https://www.dhs.gov/sites/default/files/publications/isc-risk-management-process-2016-508.pdf [accessed 5/16/18].

[ISO/IEC7816] (Parts 3:2006, 4: 2013, 5:2004, 6:2004, 8:2004, and 9:2004), *Information technology — Identification cards — Integrated circuit(s) cards with contacts.*

[ISO/IEC14443] (Parts 1:2008, 2:2010, 3:2011, and 4:2008) *Identification cards - Contactless integrated circuit(s) cards – Proximity cards.*

[M-05-24]   OMB Memorandum M-05-24, *Implementation of Homeland Security Presidential Directive 12—Policy for a Common Identification Standard for Federal Employees and Contractors*, August 2005. https://www.whitehouse.gov/sites/whitehouse.gov/files/omb/memoranda/2005/m05-24.pdf [accessed 5/16/18].

[OPM Memo]   Final Credentialing Standards for Issuing Personal Identity Verification Cards under HSPD-12, July 31, 2008 [accessed 5/16/18].

[PIV-I]   Federal CIO Council, Personal Identity Verification Interoperability For Issuers, Version 2.01, July 27, 2017. https://www.idmanagement.gov/wp-content/uploads/sites/1171/uploads/piv-i-for-issuers.pdf [accessed 5/16/18].

[RFC5280]   D. Cooper, S. Santesson, S. Farrell, S. Boeyen, R. Housley, and W. Polk, *Inter X.509 Public Key Infrastructure Certificate and Certificate Revocation List (CRL) Profile*, Internet Engineering Task Force (IETF) Network Working Group Request for Comments (RFC) 5280, May 2008. https://doi.org/10.17487/RFC5280.

[SECTION508]   *Section 508 of the Rehabilitation Act of 1973, as amended*, 29 U.S.C. §794(d), https://www.section508.gov [accessed 5/16/18].

[SKIMMER]   I. Kirschenbaum and A. Wool, "How to Build a Low-Cost, Extended-Range RFID Skimmer," *Proceedings of the 15th USENIX Security Symposium (Security '06)*, Vancouver, British Columbia, Canada, July 31 – August 4, 2006, USENIX Association: Berkeley, California, 2006, pp. 43-57. https://www.usenix.org/legacy/event/sec06/tech/full_papers/kirschenbaum/kirschenbaum.pdf [accessed 3/1/17].

[SP800-73]   NIST Special Publication 800-73-4, *Interfaces for Personal Identity Verification,* May 2015 (including updates as of 2/8/16). https://doi.org/10.6028/NIST.SP.800-73-4.

[SP800-76]   NIST Special Publication 800-76-2, *Biometric Specifications for Personal Identity Verification*, July 2013. https://doi.org/10.6028/NIST.SP.800-76-2.

[SP800-78]   NIST Special Publication 800-78-4, *Cryptographic Algorithms and Key Sizes for Personal Identity Verification*, May 2015. https://doi.org/10.6028/NIST.SP.800-78-4.

[SP800-87]   NIST Special Publication 800-87 Revision 2, *Codes for the Identification of Federal and Federally-Assisted Organizations*, April 2018. https://doi.org/10.6028/NIST.SP.800-87r2 .

[TIG SCEPACS]   *Technical Implementation Guidance: Smart Card Enabled Physical Access Control Systems, Version 2.3*, The Government Smart Card Interagency Advisory Board's Physical Security Interagency Interoperability Working Group, December 20, 2005. http://www.idmanagement.gov/tig_scepacs_v2-3/ [accessed 5/16/18]

Appendix G — Terminology

The following terms are used in this document.

Access Control	The process of granting or denying specific requests to: 1) obtain and use information and related information processing services; and 2) enter physical facilities (e.g., Federal buildings, military establishments, and border crossing entrances).
Access Control List	A list of (identifier, permissions) pairs associated with a resource or an asset. As an expression of security policy, a person may perform an operation on a resource or asset if and only if the person's identifier is present in the access control list (explicitly or implicitly), and the permissions in the (identifier, permissions) pair include the permission to perform the requested operation.
Asymmetric Keys:	Two related keys, a public key and a private key, that are used to perform complementary operations, such as authentication, encryption and decryption, signature generation and signature verification.
Assurance Level	A measure of trust or confidence in an authentication mechanism defined in terms of four levels:

- Level 1: LITTLE OR NO confidence
- Level 2: SOME confidence
- Level 3: HIGH confidence
- Level 4: VERY HIGH confidence

Authentication	The process of establishing confidence of authenticity; in this case, in the validity of a person's identity. In this publication, authentication often means the performance of a PIV authentication mechanism.
Authentication in Context	Authentication in context is a concept in which PACS may benefit from previous authentication within nested areas in a facility. The PACS may use information from previous access control decisions ("context") when making a new access control decision.
Authorization	In this publication, a process that associates permission to access a resource or asset with a person and the person's identifier(s).
Authenticator	A memory, possession, or quality of a person that can serve as proof of identity, when presented to a verifier of the appropriate kind. For example, passwords, cryptographic keys, and biometrics are authenticators.

BIO	A [FIPS201] authentication mechanism that is implemented by using a fingerprint or iris images data object sent from the PIV Card to the PACS and which is matched to the cardholder's live scan.
BIO-A	A [FIPS201] authentication mechanism in which the BIO authentication mechanism is performed in the presence of an attendant who supervises the use of the PIV Card and the submission of the PIN and the sample biometric by the cardholder.
BIO(-A)	A shorthand used throughout the document to represent both BIO and BIO-A authentication mechanisms.
Caching Status Proxy	A system used to store and re-validate certificates previously harvested from PIV cards during PACS registration. For each certificate in the cache, the proxy updates the PACS and Control Panels with the latest certificate status. The caching status proxy is usually configurable to increase or decrease the frequency with which certificates are validated.
Card UUID	The Card UUID is a UUID that is unique for each card and is a required data element on all [SP800-73] compliant PIV Cards.
Cardholder	An individual possessing an issued PIV Card.
Cardholder Unique Identifier (CHUID)	A deprecated [FIPS201] authentication mechanism or the PIV Card data object containing credential identifiers of the same name.
Cardholder UUID	The Cardholder UUID is a UUID that is a persistent identifier for the cardholder. This UUID is an optional data element on [SP800-73] compliant PIV Cards.
Certificate	A data object containing a subject identifier, a public key, and other information that is digitally signed by a certification authority. Certificates convey trust in the relationship of the subject identifier to the public key.
Certificate Revocation List	A list of revoked public key certificates created and digitally signed by a certification authority. See [RFC5280]
Certification Authority	A trusted entity that issues and revokes public key certificates.
Cloning	In this publication, a process to create a verbatim copy of a PIV Card, or a partial copy sufficient to perform one or more authentication mechanisms as if it were the original card.

Contact Reader	A smart card reader that communicates with the integrated circuit chip in a smart card using electrical signals on wires touching the smart card's contact pad. The PIV contact interface is standardized by International Organization of Standards / International Electrotechnical Commission (ISO/IEC) 7816-3 [ISO/IEC7816].
Contactless Reader	A smart card reader that communicates with the integrated circuit chip in a smart card using radio frequency (RF) signaling. The PIV contactless interface is standardized by [ISO/IEC 14443].
Controller (or Control Panel, or Panel)	A device located within the secure area that communicates with multiple PIV Card readers and door actuators, and with the Head End System. The PIV Card readers provide cardholder information to the controller, which it uses to make access control decisions and release door-locking mechanisms. The controller communicates with the Head End System to receive changes in access permissions, report unauthorized access attempts and send audit records and other log information. Most modern controllers can continue to operate properly during periods of time in which communication with the Head End is disrupted and can journal transactions so that they can be reported to the Head End when communication is restored.
	A controller is often responsible for generating challenges and verifying responses from PIV cards presented at readers. Some control panels can be configured to store certificates and their status to improve performance during authentication at the reader If not configured to store certificates and their status, a dedicated authentication controller can be used to perform challenges and responses using cached certificates. The outcome of the authentication response is then passed to the control panel in the form of the PIV card identifier, such as a FASC-N or a Card UUID.
Counterfeiting	In this publication, the creation of a fake ID card that can perform one or more authentication mechanisms, without copying a legitimate card (see Cloning).
Credential	In this publication, a collection of information about a person, attested to by an issuing authority. A credential is a data object (e.g., a certificate) that can be used to authenticate the cardholder. One or more data object credentials may be stored on the same physical memory device (e.g., a PIV Card).
Credential Validation	The process of determining if a credential is *valid*, i.e., it was legitimately issued, its activation date has been reached, it has not expired, it has not been tampered with, and it has not been

revoked, suspended, or revoked by the issuing authority.

Digital Signature	A data object produced by a digital signature method, such as Rivest, Shamir, Adleman (RSA) or the Elliptic Curve Digital Signature Algorithm (ECDSA), that when verified provides strong evidence of the origin and integrity of the signed data object.
Facility Security Committee	A committee consisting of representatives of Federal tenants in a facility, and possibly the building owner or management. The committee is responsible for building-specific security issues and approval of security policies and practices.
Federal Agency Smart Credential Number (FASC-N)	As required by [FIPS201], the FASC-N is one of the primary identifiers on the PIV Card for physical access control. The FASC-N is a fixed length (25 byte) data object, specified in [TIG SCEPACS], and included in several data objects on a PIV Card.
FASC-N Identifier	The FASC-N shall be in accordance with [TIG SCEPACS]. A subset of FASC-N, a FASC-N Identifier, is a unique identifier as described in [TIG SCEPACS]. Section 2.1, 10th paragraph of [TIG SCEPACS] states "For full interoperability of a PACS it must at a minimum be able to distinguish fourteen digits (i.e., a combination of an Agency Code, System Code, and Credential Number) when matching FASC-N based credentials to enrolled card holders." Also, Section 6.6, 3rd paragraph of [TIG SCEPACS] states, "The combination of an Agency Code, System Code, and Credential Number is a fully qualified number that is uniquely assigned to a single individual." The Agency Code is assigned to each Department or Agency by Special Publication 800-87, *Codes for the Identification of Federal and Federally-Assisted Organizations* [SP800-87]. The subordinate System Code and Credential Number value assignment is subject to Department or Agency policy, provided that the FASC-N Identifier (i.e., the concatenated Agency Code, System Code, and Credential Number) is unique for each card.
Head End System (or Access Control Server)	A system including application software, database, a Head End server, and one or more networked personal computers. The Head End server is typically used to enroll an individual's name, create a unique ID number, and assign access privileges and an expiration date. The server is also used to maintain this information and refresh the controller(s) with the latest changes. The Head End System may also be configured to host the certificate cache used by a caching status proxy. In other cases, the Head End System may include a caching status proxy.

Identifier (or Unique Identifier)	In this publication, a data object, assigned by an authority, that unambiguously identifies a person within a defined community. For example, a driver license number identifies a licensed driver within a state. The authority registers people and guarantees assignment of each identifier to a unique person.
Identity Credential	A credential that contains one or more identifiers for its subject, a person. In this publication, an identity credential is designed to verify the identity of its subject through authentication mechanisms, via an electronically mechanism (see PKI-CAK, PKI-AUTH, BIO, BIO-A, etc.).
Infrastructure	Distributed substructure of a large-scale organization that facilitates related functions or operations, e.g., telecommunications infrastructure. With regard to PACS, components include conduit, cabling, power supplies, battery backup, electrified door hardware, door position switches, and remote exit devices, as well as connectivity with other life safety systems that will ensure egress in the event of an emergency.
Interoperability	In this publication, the quality of allowing any government facility or information system to verify a cardholder's identity using the credentials on the PIV Card, regardless of the PIV Card Issuer (PCI).
Issuance (or Credential Issuance)	The process by which an issuing authority obtains and verifies information about a person, assigns one or more unique identifiers to the person, prepares information to be placed in or on a credential, produces a physical or data object credential, and delivers the finished credential to its subject. In the case of PIV Cards, issuance is performed only by accredited PCIs.
Issuer	The organization that is issuing the PIV Card to an applicant.
Multi-Factor Authentication	Authentication based on more than one factor. In some contexts, each factor is a different authenticator. In other contexts, each factor is one of "something you know, something you have, something you are" (i.e., memorized fact, token, or biometric) and thus the number of factors is 1, 2, or 3.
OCC-AUTH	A two-factor authentication mechanism that uses secure messaging and on-card comparison of cardholder fingerprint(s).
Online Certificate Status Protocol (OCSP)	An online protocol used to determine the status of a public key certificate. See [RFC2560]
PACS Registration	The process of authenticating, validating, and verifying information about the PIV cardholder prior to entering the

55

	information into a PACS server. The information added during registration is then utilized to perform authentication and authorization of an individual at an access point.
Path Validation (or Trust Path Validation)	The process of verifying the binding between the subject identifier and subject public key in a certificate, based on the public key of a trust anchor, through the validation of a chain of certificates that begins with a certificate issued by the trust anchor and ends with the target certificate. Successful path validation provides strong evidence that the information in the target certificate is trustworthy.
Personal Identification Number (PIN)	A short numeric password (6 to 8 digits) used as an authenticator by the PIV Card to authenticate the cardholder.
Personal Identity Verification (PIV) Card	A physical artifact (e.g., identity card, "smart" card) issued to an individual that contains a PIV Card Application which stores identity credentials (e.g., photograph, cryptographic keys, digitized fingerprint representation) so that the claimed identity of the cardholder can be verified against the stored credentials by another person (human readable and verifiable) or an automated process (computer readable and verifiable).
PIV System	A system comprised of components and processes that support a common (smart card-based) platform for identity authentication across Federal departments and agencies for access to multiple types of physical access environments.
Physical Access Control System (PACS)	An electronic system that controls the ability of people to enter a protected area, by means of authentication and authorization at access control points.
PKI	A support service to the PIV system that provides the cryptographic keys needed to perform digital signature-based identity verification.
PKI-AUTH	A PIV authentication mechanism that is implemented by an asymmetric key challenge/response protocol using the PIV Authentication certificate and key.
PKI-CAK	A PIV authentication mechanism that is implemented by an asymmetric key challenge/response protocol using the Card Authentication certificate and key.

(PKI-CAK | SYM-CAK) + BIO(-A)	A three-factor authentication achieved by combining BIO(-A) with either PKI-CAK or SYM-CAK. In this case, the PKI-CAK or SYM-CAK authentication mechanism is used to authenticate the PIV Card and therefore the entry of the PIN to access the biometric fingerprint template can now be trusted.
Private Key	A cryptographic key used with a public key cryptographic algorithm, which is uniquely associated with an entity, and not made public; it is used to generate a digital signature; this key is mathematically linked with a corresponding public key.
Public Key	A cryptographic key used with a public key cryptographic algorithm, uniquely associated with an entity, and which may be made public; it is used to verify a digital signature; this key is mathematically linked with a corresponding private key.
Reader	A device that interfaces with a PIV Card and a controller to execute or support execution of one or more PIV authentication mechanisms.
Relying Party	In this publication, an entity, such as a PACS, that depends upon the trust model of the PIV System to correctly produce the results of authentication, i.e., the identity of the cardholder.
Revocation	The process by which an issuing authority renders an issued credential useless. For example, a certification authority may revoke certificates it issues. Typically, a certificate is revoked if its corresponding private key is known to be, or suspected to be, compromised.
Secret Key	A key used by a symmetric key algorithm to encrypt, decrypt, sign, or verify information. In a symmetric key infrastructure (SKI), the sender and receiver of encrypted information must share the same secret key.
Secure Messaging	A protocol by which a PIV Card Application is authenticated to the relying system. Secure Messaging is used to provide confidentiality and integrity protection for the card commands that are sent to the card as for the responses from the PIV Card.
Skimming	Surreptitiously obtaining data from a contactless smart card, using a hidden reader that powers, commands, and reads from the card within the maximum read distance (reported as about 25 cm with [ISO/IEC 14443] smart cards like the PIV Card). [SKIMMER]
Sniffing	Surreptitiously obtaining data from a contactless smart card, using a hidden reader that receives RF signals from a legitimate reader and smart card when they perform a transaction. Sniffing is a form

of electronic eavesdropping. Sniffing is possible at greater distances than skimming.

Social Engineering	A process or technique, similar to a confidence game, used to obtain information from a person without raising suspicion.
SYM-CAK	The SYM-CAK is an authentication mechanism based on the optional symmetric card authentication key. As the name implies, the purpose of the SYM-CAK authentication mechanism is to authenticate the card and thereby the cardholder.
Symmetric Key	A cryptographic key that is used to perform both the cryptographic operation and its inverse, for example to encrypt and decrypt, or create a message authentication code and to verify the code.
Trust Anchor	A named entity producing digital signatures, and a corresponding certificate that a relying party has decided to trust, i.e., if a digital signature is verified using the public key within the certificate, the signature is trusted to have been made by the entity named in the certificate.
Validation	In this publication, the process of determining that an identity credential was legitimately issued and is still valid, i.e., has not expired or been revoked.
Verification	The process of determining if an assertion is true, particularly the process of determining if a data object possesses a digital signature produced by the purported signer.
VIS	A downgraded [FIPS201] authentication mechanism in which the visual identity verification of a PIV Card is done by a human guard.
Virtual Contact Interface	An interface established over the contactless interface after the presentation of the pairing code to the PIV Card using secure messaging. All non-card-management operations that are allowed over contact interface may be carried out over the VCI.
Wiegand	With regard to deployed PACS, a one-way communication protocol consisting of a formatted bit string used from the access reader to the controller. It can be used with any media, including proximity, bar code, magnetic stripe, and smart cards.

Appendix H — Abbreviations and Acronyms

ACL	Access Control List
BIO	Authentication Using Off-Card Biometric Comparison
BIO-A	Attended Authentication Using Off-Card Biometric Comparison
BIO(-A)	A short-hand to represent both BIO and BIO-A authentication mechanism
CHUID	Cardholder Unique Identifier
CRL	Certificate Revocation List
ECC	Elliptic Curve Cryptography
ECDSA	Elliptic Curve Digital Signature Algorithm
FASC-N	Federal Agency Smart Credential Number
FIPS	Federal Information Processing Standards
FISMA	Federal Information Security Modernization Act
FSL	Facility Security Level
GSA	General Services Administration
GUID	Global Unique Identification Number
HSPD	Homeland Security Presidential Directive
ID	Identification
IEC	International Electrotechnical Commission
ISC	Interagency Security Committee
ISO	International Organization for Standardization
IT	Information Technology
ITL	Information Technology Laboratory
LB	Lower Bound
NIST	National Institute of Standards and Technology
OCC	On-Card Biometric Comparison
OCC-AUTH	Authentication Using On-Card Biometric Comparison
OCSP	Online Certificate Status Protocol
OMB	Office of Management and Budget
PACS	Physical Access Control System
PCI	PIV Card Issuer
PIN	Personal Identification Number
PIV	Personal Identity Verification
PKI-AUTH	Authentication with the PIV Authentication Certificate Credential
PKI-CAK	Authentication with the Card Authentication Certificate Credential
POST	Power-on self-test
RF	Radio Frequency
RSA	Rivest, Shamir, Adleman
SP	Special Publication
SYM-CAK	Authentication with the Symmetric Card Authentication Key
UB	Upper Bound

UUID   Universally Unique Identifier

VCI   Virtual Contact Interface

VIS   Authentication using PIV Visual Credentials

Appendix I — Revision History

Version	Release Date	Updates
SP 800-116	November 2008	Initial Release
SP 800-116 Revision 1	May 2018	• Reflected [FIPS201] deprecation of CHUID authentication mechanism throughout the document. • Emphasized that while use of the CHUID authentication mechanism has been deprecated, the on-card CHUID data element has not been deprecated and continues to be mandatory. This data element is the only element with the optional Cardholder UUID. It is also used by the BIO(-A) and SYM-CAK authentication mechanisms as a source for the card's expiration date and contains unique identifiers to compare against PACS ACL entries. • Reflected downgrade of VIS authentication mechanism to LITTLE or NO" confidence in cardholder's identity in content of document. • Removed VIS + CHUID as an option to transitioning from Unrestricted to Controlled areas since it provides "LITTLE or NO" confidence in the identity of the cardholder. • Added OCC-AUTH as a two-factor authentication mechanism. • Added credential validation requirements from [FIPS201] to applicable sections of the document. • Split table on PIV Authentication Mechanism into two – one for contact and one for contactless PIV Authentication Mechanisms. • Expanded authentication in context to allow context provided by physically measures to prevent more than one person from passing through an access point (e.g., turnstiles, gates) after each authentication. This is in addition to authentication in context where PACS can store and recall recent access control decisions. • Added Appendix C – Improving PKI Authentication Transaction Times. • Expanded content of PACS registration. • Added a new section 6.1 titled "PIV Identifiers" to describe the identifiers available on the PIV Card that can map to a PACS's access control list. • Moved section 7 (PIV Authentication Mechanisms) to Appendix A. • Removed Section 9 titled "Migration Strategy" from content of document as implementation have matured and are more advanced. • Removed section 10 titled 'Future Topics'. [FIPS201] and associated special publication have addressed the future topics. The content of section 10 is now part of the document (i.e., global identifier and OCC-AUTH). • Moved Appendix C to B and added a list of authentication mechanism combinations for mechanism that have no context. • Moved Section 5 discussion on limitations of pre-PIV legacy PACS system to Appendix E. • In coordination with the Interagency Security Committee (ISC), replaced reference to the Department of Justice's "Vulnerability Assessment Report of Federal Facilities" document with the ISC's document titled "Risk Management Process for Federal Facilities" to aid deriving the security requirement for facilities. • Added Appendix I to provide an informative revision history.